The Human Tradition around the World

Series Editors

WILLIAM H. BEEZLEY, Professor of History, University of Arizona
COLIN M. MACLACHLAN, John Christy Barr Distinguished
  Professor of History, Tulane University

Each volume in this series is devoted to providing minibiographies of "real people" who, with their idiosyncratic behavior, personalize the collective experience of grand themes, national myths, ethnic stereotypes, and gender relationships. In some cases, their stories reveal the irrelevance of national events, global processes, and cultural encounters for men and women engaged in everyday life. The personal dimension gives perspective to history, which of necessity is a sketch of past experience.

The authors of each volume in this historical series are determined to make the past literal. They write accounts that identify the essential character of everyday lives of individuals. In doing so, these historians allow us to share the human traditions that find expression in these lives.

Volumes in The Human Tradition around the World Series

William B. Husband, ed. *The Human Tradition in Modern Russia* (2000).
  Cloth ISBN 0-8420-2856-0   Paper ISBN 0-8420-2857-9

K. Steven Vincent and Alison Klairmont-Lingo, eds. *The Human Tradition in Modern France* (2000). Cloth ISBN 0-8420-2804-8
  Paper ISBN 0-8420-2805-6

Anne Walthall, ed. *The Human Tradition in Modern Japan* (2001).
  Cloth ISBN 0-8420-2911-7   Paper ISBN 0-8420-2912-5

Kenneth J. Hammond, ed. *The Human Tradition in Premodern China* (2002). Cloth ISBN 0-8420-2958-3   Paper ISBN 0-8420-2959-1

Kenneth J. Andrien, ed. *The Human Tradition in Colonial Latin America* (2002). Cloth ISBN 0-8420-2887-0   Paper ISBN 0-8420-2888-9

THE HUMAN TRADITION IN
PREMODERN CHINA

THE HUMAN TRADITION IN
PREMODERN CHINA

EDITED BY

KENNETH J. HAMMOND

NUMBER 4

A Scholarly Resources Inc. Imprint
Wilmington, Delaware

Scholarly Resources Inc.
104 Greenhill Avenue
Wilmington, DE 19805-1897
www.scholarly.com

Library of Congress Cataloging-in-Publication Data

The human tradition in premodern China / edited by Kenneth J.
   Hammond.
       p. cm. — (Human tradition around the world ; no. 4)
    Includes bibliographical references and index.
       ISBN 0-8420-2958-3 (alk. paper) — ISBN 0-8420-2959-1 (pbk. :
alk. paper)
       1. China—History—Biography. 2. China—Social conditions.
I. Hammond, Kenneth J., 1949–   II. Series.

DS734 .H885 2002
951—dc21   2002017618

Acknowledgments

This book grew out of a discussion with William Beezley during a visit he made to New Mexico in 1999. I greatly appreciate his invitation to be part of the Human Tradition series. My own training and preparation for undertaking this project was most strongly shaped by my teachers at Harvard, especially Peter Bol, Philip Kuhn, and Michael Fuller, as well as by the work of established scholars such as Katy Carlitz and Ann Waltner. Obviously this book would not exist without the contributions of the chapter authors, and to them I express my gratitude and admiration for their individual efforts. My colleagues in the History Department at New Mexico State University have provided a stimulating and vital intellectual environment within which to pursue this effort. In this work, as in all things, I have been supported and encouraged most of all by my wife, Elvira, and my children, Cody, Lydia, Allison, and Willie.

About the Editor

Kenneth J. Hammond is associate professor of history at New Mexico State University. He holds a Ph.D. from Harvard University in History and East Asian Languages. He is past president of the Society for Ming Studies and is the book review editor for the Society's journal, *Ming Studies*. His field of specialization is the intellectual and cultural history of late imperial China, especially the sixteenth century.

I believe in aristocracy, though—if that is the right word, and if a democrat may use it. Not an aristocracy of power, based upon rank and influence, but an aristocracy of the sensitive, the considerate and the plucky. Its members are to be found in all nations and classes, and all through the ages, and there is a secret understanding between them when they meet. They represent the true human tradition, the one permanent victory of our queer race over cruelty and chaos. Thousands of them perish in obscurity, a few are great names. They are sensitive for others as well as for themselves, they are considerate without being fussy, their pluck is not swankiness but the power to endure, and they can take a joke.

—E. M. Forster, *Two Cheers for Democracy* (1951)

Contents

Chronology

Shang dynasty	c. 1600–1050 B.C.E.
Zhou dynasty	c. 1050–250 B.C.E.
Spring and Autumn	722–481 B.C.E.
Warring States	403–221 B.C.E.
Qin dynasty	221–207 B.C.E.
Han dynasty	204 B.C.E.–220 C.E.
Three Kingdoms	220–265
Jin dynasty	265–317
Northern and Southern dynasties	317–581
Sui dynasty	581–617
Tang dynasty	617–907
An Lushan rebellion	755–763
Five Dynasties	907–960
Liao dynasty (Khitan)	907–1125
Song dynasty	960–1279
Northern Song	960–1127
Southern Song	1127–1279
Jin dynasty (Jurchen)	1115–1234
Yuan dynasty (Mongol)	1271–1368
Ming dynasty	1368–1644
Qing dynasty	1644–1912

Introduction

Tour operators in China are fond of saying that China is a large country with a long history. This is, if anything, an understatement. Recorded history in China goes back to around 1500–1200 B.C.E., and through archaeology it is possible to make reasonable extrapolations even earlier. Thus, to undertake an overview of the broad sweep of Chinese history is always a daunting task. Subdividing Chinese history into distinct eras or periods is also a challenging endeavor. And trying to get beneath the surface of great events and major developments is yet another difficult matter.

This book is meant to be an introductory reader of biographical essays that will reveal something of the variety and complexity of human experience in China from the earliest historical times to the dawn of the modern age. Deciding where to draw the dividing line is not an easy question. For this book I have used the fifteenth century as the end point of the premodern period. By the sixteenth century the development of China's economy and society has taken on many of the characteristics that we associate with the modern world: commercialization and monetization, expanding literacy and publishing, and more extensive communication and interaction with the global economy. Early manifestations of challenges to traditional gender roles and glimmers of new forms of political organization and participation begin to appear from the sixteenth century on. Many of these phenomena can be perceived in incipient form even earlier than the Ming dynasty (1368–1644)—as early as the Southern Song dynasty (1127–1279). And, indeed, the stirrings of early modernity are disrupted in the seventeenth century by the Manchu conquest of China and the founding of the Qing dynasty (1644–1912). But the line must be drawn somewhere, and for present purposes the fifteenth century will serve us well. The early modern and modern periods will require attention of their own

Here the task is to portray the premodern period in China, which is itself divisible into smaller units of time. The essays in this book, which cover a period of about 2,700 years, can be seen as falling into three broad ages. The first is Early China, which begins with the Shang dynasty (c. 1600–1050 B.C.E.) and continues through the founding of the Han dynasty at the end of the third century B.C.E. This includes the long era of the Zhou dynasty (c. 1050–250 B.C.E.), which also encompasses the Spring and Autumn (722–481 B.C.E.) and Warring States (403–221 B.C.E.) periods and the brief but crucial Qin dynasty (221–207 B.C.E.), when China was first united under a single imperial regime. During much of the millennium and a half of Early China, warfare was the principal means of resolving political and economic conflict, and military elites were the leading forces in society. Yet it was also during this often cha- otic period that the great philosophers and thinkers of the classical tradi- tion, such as Confucius and Mencius, the Daoists Laozi and Zhuangzi, or Legalists such as Han Feizi, emerged. The ideas of these philosophi- cal founders and the impact of the power struggles of generals and kings are woven into the stories of individuals as we encounter them through- out the premodern period.

The second major age, Imperial China, begins in the Han dynasty (204 B.C.E.–220 C.E.) and continues through the Tang dynasty (617–907). This period can be broadly characterized as one in which the imperial order is consolidated, in which there is a shift in social hierarchy from the dominance of military elites to that of great aristocratic families. During the early decades of the Han the imperial state developed the essential features that would remain in place, with ongoing modifica- tions and refinements, throughout the two millennia of the Imperial age. These included a bureaucratic system of government administration and the elaboration of an ideological system combining elements of Confu- cian ethics, Legalist efficiency, and cosmological thought about the place of human society in the larger universe.

The collapse of the Tang led to the eventual rise of a new elabora- tion of Chinese society and government, the Later Imperial period, be- ginning in the Song dynasty (960–1279). The most important aspects of this new period were the development of the Confucian examination system as the core of recruitment for government service and as the cen- terpiece of elite intellectual culture, replacing the aristocratic social or- der of the Han–Tang period with one based on achievement in education, and changes in the economy of China that began a long process of com- mercialization. The growth of the examination system had broad and complex effects on social and cultural life. It gave rise to competing schools of thought in literature, philosophy, and statecraft and fueled develop- ments in painting and calligraphy. Economic change not only began to create new elites based on wealth rather than education, but also facili- tated other social transformations through the growth of the publishing industry, which made the circulation of printed texts more widespread and expanded the proportion of the population with access to written materials.

The Later Imperial period was also one in which non-Chinese peoples came to play very important roles. A series of northern frontier peoples established states that controlled parts, at first, and finally all of China. The Khitan and Jurchen occupied portions of north China from the tenth through the early thirteenth centuries, when the Mongols conquered all of China as part of their vast Eurasian empire. The challenges of these non-Chinese conquest states were a persistent problem for the civil literati bureaucrats of the imperial Chinese state throughout this final segment of the premodern age.

The essays in this book present the life stories of individuals from across this long stretch of time. Writing biographies of premodern people in China is a complicated and sometimes nearly impossible task. Although there is a long and rich tradition of historical writing in China, as well as a wealth of primary materials to supplement the written record, biography is a particularly problematic aspect of this tradition. Beginning with the work of Sima Qian, a court historian in the Han dynasty who wrote a comprehensive history of China down to the founding of the Han dynasty, biographies have formed a major component of standard historical texts. The difficulty is that the biographies included in these works differ from what we find in biographical writing today. Traditional Chinese historical writing in general was strongly influenced by a concept called "praise and blame," which was attributed to Confucius. It meant that in writing biographies of historical figures an explicit effort was made to pass moral judgement on them. Indeed, once an individual was placed into a particular moral category, his or her biography was written to illustrate the qualities and characteristics associated with that label. An evil minister would be portrayed as corrupt in all aspects of his being. A virtuous wife would be presented in terms of her complete incarnation of proper feminine morality. This kind of biographical writing does not preserve the range of materials and information generally considered desirable in modern historiography.

Nonetheless, it is possible to seek biographical knowledge of premodern China through a variety of methods. The authors of chapters in this book have followed a number of different paths in pursuit of their subjects. Minna Haapanen has combined textual sources with archaeological materials and a bit of creative synthesis to develop a dramatic presentation of the Shang dynasty royal consort Fu Hao. Based on inscriptions from the "oracle bones" used in rituals of divination, along with objects from the tomb of Fu Hao excavated in the early twentieth century, Haapanen leads us into the spiritual world of the Shang royal family as this remarkable woman might have experienced it.

Paul Goldin takes us forward to the final years of the Early China period, when the state of Qin was unifying the first true empire in China. Applying critical reading methodologies to the classic biography of the Qin chancellor Li Si from Sima Qian's *Records of the Historian*, Goldin explicates the political and philosophical processes leading to Qin's success and the central role Li Si played in those events.

Turning to a broader focus on the Cao clan, rather than one individual, Howard Goodman creates a collective biography of one of the most important families during the transitional years from the end of the Han to the Three Kingdoms period (220–265). Drawing on inscriptions, early biographical accounts, and other records from traditional historical sources, Goodman weaves an intricate narrative of political intrigue and intellectual controversy during a period that has been seen by later generations of Chinese as one of the most interesting times in their history. The aristocratic elite of clans such as the Cao dominated China for several centuries, bequeathing a stock of legendary heroes and villains to posterity.

Andy Meyer's study of Guan Lu also concerns a Three Kingdoms figure, but with an even stronger focus on the cosmological, almost magical aspects of social and political life at that time. As the Confucian order built by the Han seemed to falter with the fall of that dynasty, other schools of thought sought to determine the place of human affairs in a larger context. Chinese society was in such a state of flux during this time that individuals such as Guan Lu could rise to prominent positions outside the hegemonic hierarchy of the aristocratic clans.

The leading role of the great clans began to collapse in the later years of the Tang dynasty. Shaken by a great rebellion in the middle of the eighth century, the Tang state began to turn to new sources of talented men for service in the imperial administration. As Anthony Deblasi shows us, Quan Deyu was just such a man, rising to prominence through his literary talents and making a place for himself in official service in a period of dynastic recovery. The linkages between literary thought and politics have always been strong in China, and the career of Quan Deyu highlights this connection.

The emphasis on literary talent and literary culture as vital to good government moved from a subordinate position in the late Tang to the center stage of Chinese politics and society in the Song dynasty. The transition from Tang to Song ushered in the Late Imperial period in Chinese history, in which learning, rather than aristocratic pedigree, became the most important factor in defining social status and qualifying men for public service. The Confucian examination system became the core of elite life, shaping the educational system, the self-image of individuals, and the institutional life of the Song and later dynasties. At the same time, pressures on the Chinese states from non-Chinese peoples also became a persistent feature of life in the Late Imperial period. Rob Foster's discussion of Yue Fei points out the tensions and contradictions within Song society and politics engendered by military crisis and civil bureaucratic political interests.

While great dramas were unfolding on the stage of imperial politics, life at less prominent levels of Chinese society also went on. Anne Gerritsen moves from the wider arena of the imperial state, where the Mongol conquest of the mid-thirteenth century led to the establishment of the Yuan dynasty (1271–1368) and the marginalizing of the literati under alien rule, to the more intimate environment of local society. In her study of Liu Chenweng she sets out various ways in which a gentleman could pursue literary accomplishments and public service outside, or in the absence of, the official mechanisms of the Confucian examinations and the imperial state. By promoting what he thought of as proper Confucian values in a time when the Mongols were imposing non-Chinese ways at the imperial court and in government offices across the empire, Liu can also be seen as playing a small, but not insignificant, role in maintaining "national" consciousness and a kind of low-intensity resistance to the postconquest regime.

With the weakening of Mongol rule in the fourteenth century, and the rise of peasant-based rebellions by mid-century, the period of alien rule drew to an end. In 1368 the Ming dynasty was founded, with an ethnically Chinese ruling family headed by Zhu Yuanzhang. A strong-willed and authoritarian ruler, Zhu Yuanzhang was succeeded in 1398 by his grandson, much to the frustration of his oldest surviving son Zhu Di. In 1402, Zhu Di overthrew his nephew and seized the throne for himself. Confucian officials, who had resumed their prominent roles in government and society, were now confronted with a difficult choice: to uphold the principle of loyalty to the displaced emperor or to serve the new ruler. Peter Ditmanson tells the story of one man who faced this critical decision, and situates Fang Xiaoru's ultimate choice in the context of a life devoted to the revival of Chinese and literati values after a century of Mongol domination.

The fate of Fang Xiaoru emphasizes the return of the literati to a dominant role in Chinese society and political culture. But the Ming dynasty was one of increasing dynamism and diversity, and the Confucian scholars had to share the stage with rivals for political power and social prestige. Kenneth Hammond discusses one group that contended with the literati from a special position within the inner chambers of the imperial palace. Eunuchs such as Wang Zhen could sometimes build positions of great power on their intimate access to emperors and their control of daily affairs in the imperial residence. The influence Wang Zhen exercised over a young emperor from 1435 to 1449 greatly discomfited the officials of the regular civil bureaucracy. But despite his ultimate fall, eunuchs remained a force the literati had to contend with for the rest of the Ming period.

Outside the ranks of imperial administration, Ming society was also undergoing great changes as the commercial sector of the economy became increasingly important. As early as the Song dynasty, some families had begun to accumulate great fortunes through mercantile activity, and in the Ming this process resumed and accelerated. Ina Asim's brief study of one such merchant, rather confusingly with the same name as the eunuch in the previous chapter, shows how traditional social categories and hierarchies began to disintegrate by the middle years of the Ming. Asim draws heavily on evidence from Wang's tomb, bringing us in some ways back to the kinds of biographical evidence with which Minna Haapanen began her chapter on Fu Hao of so many centuries before.

The stories of individuals and families included in this book are by no means an exhaustive or comprehensive portrayal of premodern Chinese society. The vast complexity of space and time encompassed in the history of China before the sixteenth century would require multiple volumes to address. Here we have attempted to present a group of lives that reveal basic features of Chinese society and political culture, going beneath the surface of great figures like emperors and of philosophers such as Confucius to touch on more "ordinary" persons. And yet, given the nature of the sources available through these many centuries, virtually all of the individuals considered here have come from the social elite. The voices of peasants and artisans, and to a large extent of women of all classes, remain largely unheard.

CHAPTER I

The Royal Consort
Fu Hao of the Shang

Circa 1200 B.C.E.

MINNA HAAPANEN

Chinese society emerges in the historical record during the Shang dynasty, a period beginning around 1700 B.C.E. and continuing to 1045 B.C.E. About halfway between these dates, written records suddenly become quite numerous. The great bulk of these are inscriptions on two kinds of objects; the shoulder bones of cattle or the plastrons (undershells) of turtles. These objects were used in rituals through which the rulers of the Shang state consulted their deceased ancestors, the former kings, about a wide variety of subjects, from the prospects for harvests to the advisability of military campaigns. Carefully preserved by burial near the Shang capital city at Anyang in central China, tens of thousands of these "oracle bones" have been excavated by archaeologists in the twentieth century.

Drawing on these unique primary sources, Minna Haapanen, a doctoral candidate at the Cotsen Institute of Archaeology at the University of California at Los Angeles, specializing in the study of the Shang, has constructed a biographical portrait of Fu Hao, consort to the Shang king Wu Ding, who reigned around 1200 B.C.E. Ironically, Fu Hao is one of the few women in premodern China about whom it is possible to develop this kind of information. Her tomb has been excavated, and knowledge derived from that process has supplemented the written record to give a fuller image of her life and times.

In this chapter, Haapanen combines citations from the original inscriptions with her own speculative reconstruction of Fu Hao's life events, presented in the first-person voice. The recorded divinations take the form of dated entries, using a complex calendar system of sixty days marked by terms such as jisi *or* xinwei *(days), and also including the year within the reign of the king in whose name the inscription was made. Based on our present knowledge of early Chinese history, we cannot correlate these to specific dates in the Western calendar.*

The story of Fu Hao's life as a royal consort, and the spiritual and political world she inhabited, forms the starting point of China's recorded

1

history and provides a window into the society and economy of this earliest phase in Chinese civilization.

The air was moist and hot and I could smell the marshes to the east. At this time of year, plants had already started to rot. The smell of rotten leaves and roots mixed with vapors rose from the still water. As the wind turned, a faint scent of marsh flowers reached me. I breathed it in and enjoyed the relief it gave. The moisture in the air prevented me from seeing the Mountains before me. They were definitely there; so many times I had admired them and so many times I had cursed their existence on my way to the Northwest. I was riding in my carriage towards the Settlement. I had been away for quite a long time, too long some said. It was time to go back and rest.

To reach the palace I had to pass the bronze, bone, and jade workshops. The wind blew from the River and I smelled the burning coal in the furnaces, molten bronze being poured to the molds, and the sweat of the workers. Even though I had lived in the Settlement for years, I had never gotten used to the smell of molten bronze. Every time it hit my nostrils, I could feel it creeping down to my lungs and nearly choking me. As I passed the workshops, the noises coming from them overshadowed every other sound. I could only hear the River after I had passed the pit dwellings and as I was approaching the palace.

On the day jisi in the 4th moon of the 6th year of Wu Ding

I cannot comprehend why we have to have this argument time and time again. He knows as well as I do that I have been trained to attack our enemies and punish them. This is what I want to do, and this is what the situation requires. He accuses me of being disrespectful towards him. How dare he! Our Ancestors know that I am needed. I am the granddaughter of Nan Geng, the wife of the King. They have faith in their descendant. They have watched over my training and prepared me for these journeys; why would they disapprove of me this time?

Finally, I gave in. Tomorrow I will prepare the bones.

On the day xinwei in the 4th moon of the 6th year of Wu Ding

Just as I thought! As the King read the cracks he became convinced that there is no reason for this delay. The bones approve of this campaign, so he will let me leave. Fortunately I had already prepared my men for departure. I will head towards the northwest tomorrow. Zhi Guo will meet me at the Pass.

I was born on the day Dingwei, 2nd moon of the first year of Xiang Jia and named Tu of the clan of Zi. I was raised to be one of the *fus* [consorts] in the King's court. My parents made sure that I had the necessary education to live the life of a queen. They expected much from me. Before me, the *fus* coming from the Zi clan had always been known for their loyalty, courage, and abilities. My parents wanted to make sure that I would not disgrace them. And I didn't.

On the day xinmao in the 9th moon of the 6th year of Wu Ding

The battle is over. My men fought bravely. They have learned to work well with Zhi Guo's troops. We had some disagreements over the tactics. I was sure that his plan to use the same battle formation used against the Zhou would not be successful. After all, the Tu are a completely different tribe. He said that these barbarians were all the same; the house of Shang would always reign. This time, at least, he was right. I sent him back to the Settlement to present the war captives to the King. I will go and rest at my ancestral house.

My father belonged to the family of Nan Geng. I was raised on our family estate which is a day's journey to the east from Yan, Nan Geng's capital. Our dwelling was near the riverbed surrounded by forests and fields of millet. The forests were rich with animals; on most days we could enjoy deer and boar meat. Occasionally we even encountered leopards, tigers, and rhinos. It was so different then: now we are lucky just to get a glimpse of a rhino.

My father enjoyed hunting. He often took me and my younger brother with him. I remember the day I was able to present my first catch to our Ancestors. It was only a small rabbit, but I was so proud! My mother was standing beside me while I prepared the rabbit as a meal for her to present in the family shrine. I was old enough to prepare the meal, but not quite old enough to enter the shrine.

On the day xinhai in the 9th moon of the 6th year of Wu Ding

Everything seems to be in order. My younger brother has taken good care of our home. He has been able to find artisans so skillful that even the King is envious of them. He presented the latest products of our workshops yesterday. The Ancestors will be pleased with the vessels! According to my wishes, he had started to prepare my funerary vessels as well. He wasn't happy when I gave the order. He does not understand that I need a burial worthy of a representative of the Zi clan when I become an Ancestress. I have to show respect towards my parents and my Ancestors. They have made me who I am.

When I was a little girl, the Settlement was only a small village. It was Pan Geng who moved the capital to the foot of the Mountains, to the north of the Great River. People were not pleased with him, but there wasn't much they could do; after all, he was the King. I remember the first day I entered it. There was not much there then; it did not even have city walls like Ao had. There were no royal buildings nor temples, only ordinary dwellings. It still doesn't have walls, but now it looks more like a capital. Wu Ding is truly a great king. It began to look like a capital only gradually. The King built palaces and temples, established workshops, and forced the nobility to settle there permanently. Once he had accomplished this, the area started to grow as the nobles' residences spread outwards and as the workers settled into their crowded villages. Goods started to flow in from all four lands: copper and tin for the ritual vessels, coal for the furnaces, and turtle plastrons for the bones. The King wanted the palace and the temples to be close to each other. With help from the Ancestors, he decided to erect them where the waters bend. We lived in the northern part of the compound closest to the River. It did not take as long to build our palace as it did to build the temples. First the location and direction of the temple buildings were set by the bones. Then the ground on which they were built was sanctified and the proper sacrifices were performed. These were tiresome months for the King and for the diviners helping him. Nothing could be left to chance; everything had to have our Ancestors' consent.

The palace the King built for us looked magnificent in the morning sun. I often stood on the main stairs and looked towards the River. No matter how early I was, there I always saw people going about their business. I could see the fishermen along the banks of the River, coming back from the night's fishing. They held their precious fishing birds gently on one arm and carried their catches with the other. The women from the kitchens met them halfway and took the fish from them. Even though they were a long way from me, I could hear them talking. Later in the morning, I could see the dyers with heavy rolls of silk on their shoulders heading towards the River. They would spend the whole day dyeing the silk.

On the day yichou in the 2nd moon of the 9th year of Wu Ding

I had a fretful dream last night! I begged the King to find out if it was caused by Father Yi. He has never forgiven my mother's sister for her disrespectfulness towards the Ancestors of the house of Zi, and especially towards him. She should not have favored her relatives in such a way, no matter how powerful diviners they might have once been. Now that I am the only living female member of my mother's house, he wants me to rectify the situation.

On the day dingmao in the 2nd moon of the 9th year of Wu Ding

The bones told us that my dream was indeed caused by Father Yi. The King demands that I offer sacrifices to Father Yi in order to appease him. Tomorrow I will sacrifice sheep and pigs to him and hope that I can undo the damage done by my mother's sister. . . .

I was six *sui* when my mother started to teach me how to prepare sacrifices to our Ancestors. By that time it was already known that I should become one of the *fus* of the future king. My mother harbored ambitions of my even becoming a queen some day, so she took great care in preparing me for the duties of a queen. I learned how to prepare bones for divination as well as how to prepare whole sacrificial meals. Every sacrifice has strict rules of how they should be prepared. There are several possible combinations of meat, wheat, and vegetable dishes. I had to learn which ones were proper for each individual occasion since funerary rituals required combinations different from the yearly sacrifices to the Ancestors, the Powers, and to Di. I made many mistakes and my mother did not hesitate to punish me. All that I wanted to do was to practice military skills with my father and my younger brother. The slaps on my fingers and wrists did not help to direct my concentration to my mother's words and instructions. She soon realized that the only way to make me learn was to promise to let me join my father and brother if I did well. After we finished inside, my mother often joined us. She enjoyed riding in a carriage as much as I did.

On the day renwu of the 1st moon of the 10th year of Wu Ding

This time I am desperate to have a son! The King deserves an heir, and I want to be the one to provide him with it. My son has to be the next king! I owe that to my family and to my Ancestors.

On the day jiashen in the 1st moon of the 10th year of Wu Ding

This pregnancy is different from the other ones. Ever since the 11th moon I have had pains that have sometimes even confined me to my bed for days. I hope it is just the cold, but I know the King is worried.

My father was a great man. He never became king even though his father had been the head of the house of Shang. Instead, his cousins Pan Geng, Xiao Xin, and Xiao Yi, each in his turn, held the banner and the battle-ax as the rulers of Shang. My father never complained. He served the kings with utmost loyalty and he was well respected among the noblemen of Shang.

On the day guiwei in the 3rd moon of the 10th year of Wu Ding

Minister Yue visited me today. He hoped that I would feel better soon. The childbirth was not good, just as the Ancestors said it would not be. Now it is time for me to return to my duties. I shall have better fortune next time.

The King could not have a better minister. I know that I can trust him to give the best advice to the King while I am away. I know he thinks highly of me as well. He said that I am worthy of my Name. He knows me well enough to know what kind of compliments I like the best!

I married the King when I was 15 *sui*. By that time he had already been a king a few years and I had been in court since my 10th birthday. His father had died suddenly and he had spent three years in mourning. His ministers were worried about him. I had heard about his behavior and felt that I was truly marrying a man worthy of the banner of Shang. So, as I entered the marriage I did not feel frightened. My mother and father had prepared me for that day, and I knew that from that moment on I would be able to fulfill their expectations.

He waited for me in front of our dwelling. The ceremony was not too lavish. Neither of us wanted that. It was a simple feast, just enough to bring honor to our Ancestors. People, of course, drank a lot of ale, but that is the way the Zi do things. The first time I met Minister Yue was at the ceremony. He had joined the king a year earlier and had already helped the King to regulate the state. We immediately had veneration for each other. I knew that this was going to be a fruitful cooperation.

On the day yiyou in the 3rd moon of the 13th year of Wu Ding

Everyone is pleased that I finally gave the clan a son. No one could be more pleased than me: I have finally fulfilled my duties towards the Ancestors. *Son*

The King gave me copper and tin, silk, and jade as a token of his gratitude. I asked my brother to use the metal for my funerary vessels. Next time I visit my ancestral house, I will present the silk to my Ancestors. It is beautiful silk. My mother and my grandmother are going to value it.

My father gave me 3,000 well trained men when I got married. The noblemen at the Settlement were impressed by my father's generosity and in awe that such an inspiring force should be delighted to follow me. They did not realize how well my father had taught me. I did not have to wait for long to show that I was able to live up to my Name.

The King was anxious to expand his territory, but he lacked the necessary military force. Minister Yue had seen me with my men training in the fields outside the Settlement and so he recommended sending me to face the Gong Fang. The King thought the Gong Fang an easy enemy for me to prove myself against and so he sent me to face them. The Gong Fang were no match for our royal carriages and bronze halberds. Their lines fell into confusion and their forces withdrew as soon as they saw the front forces of our army. The noblemen back at the Settlement finally understood my father.

On the day yiyou in the 8th moon of the 19th year of Wu Ding

I do not feel well. I have been this way ever since we came back from the hunt. The King suspects that Long Si has something to do with it. Maybe she is envious of me. I requested the King to ask the Ancestors what I should do. I would like to go to the ancestral house and rest there for a while, but I am afraid to travel when I am feeling like this.

On the day dinghai in the 8th moon of the 19th year of Wu Ding

It was Long Si. We sacrificed pigs and sheep to her. We hope she will stop tormenting me now. The bones approve of my going, and no harm will come upon me. The King is still worried, but I have faith in the divination. I shall leave at dawn.

Fighting battles for the King was easy. The hardest work was to please the people at court. My mother had taught me how to be a queen. They thought so well of me that some people said I was too much of a queen. When I first was married, I tried so hard to please everyone. I soon learned that it could not be done. Minister Yue guided me and showed me who was worthy of my trust. After a while I learned not to make mistakes.

On the day dingyou in the 9th moon of the 19th year of Wu Ding

The journey was difficult and straining. It was so hot that the horses were not able to run as fast as usual. Although I feel exhausted, I am relieved to be here. My brother's wife takes care of me. She is very respectful towards me even though I have called her my sister several times now.

On the day dingmao in the 10th moon of the 19th year of Wu Ding

I guess the journey was harder than I expected. I have been sick for a whole moon now. Even the King came to see me. He made me promise that I would get better. The King said that Minister Yue and he himself both need me. Even if I would like to comply with the King's wishes, my recovery is not in my hands. I asked the King to divine and sacrifice on my behalf.

It was hard work earning the respect of the King's ministers, but even harder was the life among his women. Every one of them knew that my role was different from theirs, although it was not so in the beginning. Just like them, I had been only one *fu* among many. The King, however, soon realized the value of my exceptional upbringing and grew greatly attached to me. The bond between us and the effects it had on my life made it difficult for the other women to accept me after the marriage took place. Yet again, Minister Yue helped me. He made me see that even though my role was special, they had a role to fulfill as well, and I should not behave disrespectfully towards any one of them.

On the day wuchen in the 12th moon of the 19th year of Wu Ding

It has never taken so long for me to recover from anything, even childbirth. Maybe I am getting old. . . .

Slowly, I have been trying to resume part of my duties here at court. Soon is the time for the annual Spring sacrifice. I am glad that I feel up to performing it. I have not missed this sacrifice since I came to the Settlement.

My greatest enemies among the women were the ones who came from the great diviner families. Their power was enormous and they felt I was a threat to them. It took me many years to prove that I was not after that kind of power. I was not interested in the power struggles between the great families or in the petty disputes that were always present at court. My only goal was to serve the King and my family and thereby bring honor to my Ancestors.

On the day jiyou in the 5th moon of the 20th year of Wu Ding

I have not been the same since the sickness. The days at the battlefield are over for me. The troubles with the Tu and the Gong have been greatly reduced in number since our early days. Now I take care of the routine matters here at the Settlement; I still perform sacrifices and prepare bones for divinations. When the King is here he often takes me hunting. The trips are not as long as they once were, but at least I get to see one of those magnificent and powerful tigers running from the party as the beast is chased out of the brush. I can see the muscles under its skin, the gleaming eyes filled with anger and fear as it approaches us. As my spear reaches the target, I can see the blood coming from its chest when it falls to the ground, sweat running along its sides and steam rising from the open wound, as the warm blood slowly drips to the soil. It is defeated.

There are still people at court of whom my family has to be wary. There is not anything they would not do to get the King to disown my children, but as long as they have Minister Yue standing beside them I do not have to worry.

On the day jiazi in the 6th moon of the 21st year of Wu Ding

I have not visited the Great City Shang in a long time, not since my father became an Ancestor. It has not seemed important since the Settlement is where the King spends most of his time. I should have taken the time to come here. All the old noble families still have some of their descendants living here and this is where the early kings of our clan are buried. I still feel the same solemn peace I felt when I used to come here with my father. He pointed out all the tombs to me and told me stories about our clan founder Xie, and about the days Da Yi defeated the tyrannical Xia and founded our lineage.

I enjoyed my life at the Settlement. I fulfilled my duties as a respectful daughter: I fought the King's battles and, above all, I gave life to three daughters and a son. Only one girl and the son, however, survived the early years of their lives. I supervised their education and made sure that both of them learned the proper respect towards their Ancestors and towards their clan.

On the day guiyou in the 8th moon of the 21st year of Wu Ding

I feel tired. The heat of the summer is bothering me, and the smell of the marshes and the sounds from the River seem too much to bear. The King has been divining about my health for days now. The Ancestors do not answer. Have they deserted me?

On the day *wuzi*, in the 11th moon of the 21st year of the King, I became an Ancestress. They buried my body to the southwest of the Palace. I wanted my body to be buried across the River where the King would lie when his time should come, but he had insisted that he wanted me close even when I was gone. My funerary procession left from the palace at dawn. They placed my body in front, on a horse-drawn carriage. My body was dressed in bright yellow and red silk woven by my daughter, my brother's wife, and their daughters. Behind the carriage was the King. I was horrified to see that he was not riding in his carriage but walking among the others. I could hear everyone in the crowd sighing and whispering with respect. Women in the crowd began to wail as the funerary procession neared my tomb. Soon the wailing filled the air and I no longer could hear the River. A maid supported the Minister Yue who seemed so much older than when I had seen him last. My lacquered coffin was lowered to the center chamber, and my closest servants, along with the slaves and dogs, were buried around my coffin. They also buried most of my possessions, including the beautiful knives and mirrors I had brought back with me from my journeys to the Northwest. They included everything I need in my new life as an Ancestress. They gave me cowrie shells for wealth and bronzes for ancestor rituals. The workshops at my ancestral house had worked day and night to produce these ever since my brother had heard the news I was ill. The King had bronzes

made with my ancestral name inscribed on them. From that day on-
wards I have been known as Mother Xin.

~

This narrative details the possible life of Fu Hao, who was one of the
consorts (*fus*) of Wu Ding, the twenty-first king of the Shang dynasty
(c. 1600–1050 B.C.E.). The traditional historical sources of China, such
as the *Shi jing*, the *Shang shu*, and the *Shi ji*, do not mention Fu Hao. The
most comprehensive written sources we have on her are oracle-bone
inscriptions and Shang divination records inscribed on bovine scapulae
and turtle plastrons, where her name is mentioned several times. The
oracle-bones also refer to other women, other *fus*. According to the current view, the *fus* were consorts of Shang kings who may or may not have
been sexually tied to the ruler (Keightley 1999: 30). Their role and functions in the Shang society varied, depending on, presumably, their social
and political connections as well as on their personal relationship with
the king in power.

The names of the consorts appearing in the oracle-bone record are
considered to consist of two parts (Chang 1980: 190). The first part is
the character *fu*, which means consort or wife. The second character is
considered to be the name of the clan from which the *fu* in question
came. Here I have followed Chang Chen-lang's (1983: 103) theory,
according to which the name "Hao" consisted of the word "Zi," the
clan name of the ruling house of Shang, and of a radical meaning a
woman. So her name here reads as "Lady from the clan of Zi." Her first
name in this story is Tu, which is derived from the inscriptions on the
bronze vessels that were buried with her (Chang Ping-ch'üan 1983: 126–
27).

This narrative is a mixture of various lines of evidence as well as of
various theories about the Shang ruling apparatus and about Fu Hao.
Therefore, the impression I give of her and of the Shang period might
not be considered orthodox, and requires an explanation of which parts
of the story are based on what kind of evidence and which are solely
the fruit of my imagination. The sources given here are mostly general
Western-language introductions, most of which then supply more comprehensive bibliographies.

I have inferred most of the information concerning her life from the
oracle-bone inscriptions. The Fu Hao inscriptions can be divided into
four general categories: (1) Inscriptions pertaining to the person of Fu
Hao, in which category there are three topics: child-bearing, Fu Hao's
health, and Fu Hao's dreams. (2) Topics related to Fu Hao's role in Shang
religion. This category consists of several sacrificial divinations, such as

HJ 2617 and HJ 2613, where Fu Hao performs a sacrifice to a particular ancestor.* The socket notation of Fu Hao ritually preparing a bone also belongs to this category. (3) Topics related to Fu Hao's military role, and (4) Inscriptions with the formula: divine/it is/ancestor X/obtain/Fu or Fu Hao. The references to her military role, child-bearing, and her role in the Shang religious life are based on the above oracle-bones.

The description of her funeral and her tomb is based on her tomb, which was found in Anyang in 1976 (Chang 1980: 87–88). It was a vertical shaft with an opening half a meter belowground. The opening of the tomb was 5.6 meters north-south and 4 meters east-west. The tomb was 7.5 meters deep with the walls sloping slightly inward. About 6.3 meters below the opening, there was a ledge 0.3 meters wide and 1.3 meters high around the tomb pit. Just above the ledge there was a long niche on both the east and west walls. The niches were used to house part of the sacrificial victims, the total number of whom was sixteen. The coffin was put in the bottom of the grave, with a waist pit underneath it. In the waist pit were a skeleton of a dog and a human (Chang 1980: 87–88). Although this tomb was much smaller than the ones found on the other side of the Huan River, it yielded the best assemblage of grave goods so far found in Anyang, because it had not been looted. Altogether more than 1,600 objects and 7,000 cowrie shells were found. Among the objects, there were more than 440 bronzes, more than 590 jades, over 560 bone objects, in excess of 70 stone objects, several ivory carvings, several pottery objects, shell objects, and three seashells (Chang 1980: 88).

For descriptions of the Settlement, that is, the Shang archaeological site at Anyang in Henan province, at various stages of her life, I relied on archaeological evidence. Here I refer the reader to such general descriptions as Chang Kwang-chih's *Shang Civilization* and to Bagley's (1999) article in the *Cambridge History of Ancient China*. These studies will also direct interested readers to primary sources. Descriptions of fauna present in the area at that time and of its climate are based on archaeological evidence, too. Such matters as Fu Hao's genealogy, place of birth, dates, age at marriage and at death, as well as her character and temperament, are inferences created from the author's knowledge of the period and its historical context.

---

*"HJ" refers to Guo Moruo, ed., and Hu Houxian, ed. in chief, *Jiaguwen heji*, 13 vols., 1978–82, which is a collection of oracle-bone inscriptions. The number refers to the number of the particular inscription in that collection. These inscriptions can also be found in Yao Xiaosui and Xiao Ding, eds., *Yinxu Jiagu Keci Leizuan*, 3 vols., Beijing, 1989, with the same HJ numbers, pp. 183 ff.

SUGGESTED READINGS

Bagley, Robert. "Shang Archaeology." In *The Cambridge History of Ancient China. From the Origins of Civilization to 221 B.C.*, edited by Michael Loewe and Edward L. Shaugnessy, 124–231. Cambridge, 1999.

Chang, Kwang-chih. *Shang Civilization*. New Haven, 1980.

_____, ed. *Studies of Shang Archaeology. Selected Papers from the International Conference on Shang Civilization*. New Haven, 1983.

Keightley, David N. *Sources of Shang History. The Oracle-Bone Inscriptions of Bronze Age China*. Berkeley, 1978.

_____. "At the Beginning: The Status of Women in Neolithic and Shang China." *Nan nü: Women and Gender in Early and Imperial China* 1 (1999): 1–63.

_____. *Ancestral Landscape: Time, Space, and Community in Late Shang China, Ca. 1200–1045 B.C.* China Research Monographs. Berkeley, 2000.

Li Chi. *Anyang: A Chronicle of the Discovery, Excavation, and Reconstruction of the Ancient Capital of the Shang Dynasty*. Seattle, 1977.

Shaugnessy, Edward L. "Historical Geography and the Extent of the Earliest Chinese Kingdoms." In *Asia Major*, 3d ser., 2:1–22.

CHAPTER 2

Li Si

Chancellor of the Universe

Paul Rakita Goldin

A thousand years passed between the life of Fu Hao and the life of Li Si. During that time the Shang dynasty was replaced by the Zhou, which at first largely replicated the political and social order of the Shang. But by about the eighth century B.C.E., the Zhou polity began to fragment, and Zhou society began a long period of change and development. From the fifth through the third century B.C.E., China came to be divided into a number of "warring states," from which this period in its history takes its name. The Warring States era ended in 221 B.C.E. with the unification of China under the leadership of Qin Shihuangdi, the First Emperor of Qin. The name China comes from this time. Qin was the strongest of the Warring States and brought about unification through a combination of force and diplomacy. Central to the success of Qin was the doctrine of Legalism, which relied upon the use of rewards and punishments to enforce order and discipline throughout the government and society.

Li Si was one of the most important figures in the success of the Qin. Paul Goldin, assistant professor of history at the University of Pennsylvania and the author of Rituals of the Way *and* The Culture of Sex in Ancient China, *presents an overview of Li's life based primarily on the account given in the classic* Records of the Historian, *written a little more than a century after the events took place. Goldin uses the career of Li Si to trace out the final stages of the rise of Qin and to portray the tangle of philosophical and political ideas and practices that combined to enable the Qin to overcome all rivals and achieve the unification of the first true empire in Chinese history.*

Almost all of our information concerning Li Si (c. 280–208 B.C.E.), the great Chancellor of the Qin Empire, comes from his biography in the magisterial *Records of the Historian*, by Sima Qian (145?–86? B.C.E.).[1] It is remarkable that were it not for this one document, we could say virtually nothing about one of the most pivotal figures in Chinese history. As it is, our view of Li Si is inevitably colored by the biases of Sima Qian, who, notwithstanding his deserved fame as a historian, incorporated into his writings a peculiar view of the empire and its legitimacy. Still, the extant biography of Li Si admirably conveys his historical importance and furnishes a prism through which posterity can observe the momentous events accompanying the rise and fall of the Qin Empire.

We are told nothing more of Li Si's origins than that he was born to a family of commoners from Shangcai, in the state of Chu, and served as a minor functionary in the local administration. An amusing anecdote explains why Li Si was unsatisfied with this humble post: "He saw that the rats in the latrines and the functionaries' quarters ate refuse, and would always be terrified whenever people or dogs approached. When [Li] Si entered the granary, he observed that the rats in the granary ate mounds of grain, and, living under a great portico, were not bothered by people or dogs. Therefore Si sighed and said: 'People are worthy or ignoble just like rats: [one's fate] depends on where one is located!' "

In the context of Li Si's biography, the apparent significance of this story is that it reveals the ambition of an undistinguished government clerk who would go on to become one of the most powerful men in all of China. However, Sima Qian was concerned with the question of why the virtuous suffer and the iniquitous prosper, and frequently used the commonplace of "success or failure depend on one's circumstances." So this quotation may also be intended to show that Li Si had profound insight into the reality of life.

Next we read that Li Si became a student of the renowned scholar Xun Qing (or Xunzi) in order to master "the techniques of an emperor or king" and thus prepare himself for a more glorious political career.[2] This period of apprenticeship must have taken place between the years 255 B.C.E., when Xunzi was appointed Magistrate of Lanling (in Chu), and 247 B.C.E., when Li Si left Chu to seek his fortunes in the mighty state of Qin. Evidently sensing that his teacher was no longer useful to him, Li Si bade farewell: "I have heard that one must seize the moment and not be idle," he says, adding that he will find employment at the court of the King of Qin, who is about to conquer the world.

In Qin, Li Si found favor with Lü Buwei, who was Chancellor and—so Sima Qian alleges—the illegitimate father of Zheng, then King of Qin and later First Emperor. With such a lofty patron, Li Si was granted the opportunity to speak to the King and seems to have excited him with hortatory flattery, asserting that victory and unprecedented power were within his Majesty's grasp. The King then followed many of Li Si's specific suggestions, which involved bribing those of his enemies who could be bribed and assassinating those who could not.

Some years later, in 237 B.C.E., Li Si faced his first political challenge: a faction at the Qin court, motivated more by fear of espionage than by xenophobia, urged the King to banish all foreigners currently serving in the Qin government. Li Si, as a native of Chu, would have been expelled under this resolution, so he argued against it in a flowery memorial that Sima Qian has preserved in its entirety, presumably as an example of effective rhetoric. In this oration, Li Si recalls several former rulers of Qin who employed foreign advisers, but the section that the hedonistic king must have found most persuasive discusses the many wonders and treasures that he has imported from alien lands—of which "the sultry girls of Zhao" were not the least delightful. It is incongruous that a king with such international tastes should consider banishing all the foreigners in his state. "You would seem to care more for sex, music, and gems than you do for people."

The King had to relent, of course, because the proposal was incompatible with his own imperialistic aspirations. A ruler of the world had to be more than just the ruler of Qin. In taking such a prominent role in this debate, Li Si emerged as one of the leading politicians in the Qin court, and rose rapidly through the ranks to the post of Commandant of Justice (comparable in power, perhaps, to the attorney general of the United States, but with far greater influence on policy making).

That same year, Li Si is said to have encouraged the King of Qin to annex the neighboring state of Han "in order to intimidate the other states." When Li Si arrived in Han to declare Qin's intentions, the King of Han was understandably upset and asked his relative Han Fei—another former student of Xunzi—to save Han by diplomatic means. (Han Fei's surname is identical to that of his native state.) At this juncture, the details become sketchy. All sources agree that Han Fei was imprisoned in Qin and forced to commit suicide in 233 B.C.E., and that the state of Han was annihilated in the same year. Beyond that, events are difficult to reconstruct.

The Annals of the First Emperor of Qin in *Records of the Historian* inform us that Han Fei did not arrive in Qin until 233, four full years after Li Si first threatened the King of Han. No extant sources explain what transpired in the interim.[3] Moreover, the surviving works of Han Fei (known as the *Han Feizi*) include a number of documents pertaining to this affair that raise more questions than they answer. There is a memorial by Han Fei in which he argues that it is in Qin's own best interest to preserve the state of Han, as well as a rebuttal by Li Si contending that an independent Han is like an infirmity of the heart or stomach plaguing Qin. Li Si goes on to outline a complex plan: he begs leave to return to Han in order to delude their king into thinking that Qin will aid its former enemy, whereupon Qin will seize the opportunity and conquer Han once and for all. Then there is a third set of memorials, ostensibly recording Li Si's duplicitous speeches to the King of Han.

But the situation is confused further by yet another memorial in the *Han Feizi*; here Han Fei addresses the King of Qin, urging him to become a "hegemon" by destroying the other states—including Han, Han Fei's own homeland! We must conclude either that one or more of these documents are spurious, or that Han Fei recognized the inevitable and switched his allegiance from Han to Qin. This change of heart would explain why it is alleged in Han Fei's biography that Li Si slandered Han Fei, caused him to be imprisoned on a trumped-up charge, and finally inveigled him into killing himself. The King of Qin, we are told, was impressed by Han Fei's writings and must have been contemplating his potential value as a minister of Qin. Thus Li Si may have considered Han Fei—whom he would have known, after all, from the days when they were both studying under Xunzi—as a dangerous rival and plotted to have him removed.

For the next two decades, Li Si's place in the Qin government was secure. When the King of Qin united China in 221 B.C.E. and declared himself the First Emperor, Li Si, as Commandant of Justice of the entire empire, had already attained more success than he could ever have imagined while contemplating the rats in the functionaries' privy at Shangcai—and as one of the new emperor's most trusted advisers, his future promised even greater dignities and honors.

On the other hand, history has not preserved the names of every commandant of justice in ancient China, and if it were not for Li Si's activities *after* the founding of the empire, he would hardly be remembered today. Li Si's first opportunity to influence the complexion of imperial government came soon after the King of Qin assumed the title of "Emperor" (*huangdi*) in 221. The chancellor, a man named Wang Wan, suggested that the sons of the Emperor be granted fiefs so as to assist in the administration of the Emperor's vast new realm. We are told that all the other ministers concurred with this opinion, but Li Si opposed it. He pointed out that the idea of dividing the realm into fiefs entrusted to relatives or trusted allies of the sovereign was obviously taken directly from the model of the Zhou and that it should not take much reflection to realize that the protracted period of warfare from which China had only just emerged was the consequence of this very practice. Only a few generations after the establishment of the Zhou dynasty, the various feudal lords were able to cast off the yoke of its suzerainty and rule their fiefs as independent states. It was therefore quite imprudent for the new emperor to follow the policies of the dynasty that he had just replaced. The King agreed: "It is because there were marquises and princes that the world has been collectively embittered by ceaseless warfare. . . . If we re-establish [feudal] principalities, this will be sowing strife; will it not be difficult to find peace in this [strategy]? The proposal of the Commandant of Justice is correct."

In place of the old feudal covenants, the First Emperor inaugurated an administrative system that revealed a fundamentally different conception of the empire—one that had been adumbrated by earlier political thinkers, but had never been instituted on such a prodigious scale. The realm was divided into thirty-six "commanderies" governed by a bureaucratic administration under the direct control of the emperor himself. Then all the weapons in the empire were supposedly collected, melted down, and recast into bells and statues. The powerful families of the vanquished kingdoms were forcibly relocated to the new imperial capital, and simulacra of their palaces were built in the capital as well.

We are not told whether Li Si had a role in these particular reforms, but they are plainly in line with the imperialist vision for which he was becoming famous. Already in 237 B.C.E., his memorial against the proposal to banish foreigners from Qin disclosed his view of the state as an entity that transcended regional differences by incorporating equally all the territories of the world. One might argue that because Li Si himself was an alien dwelling in Qin, this speech was written more out of self-interest than from any grandiose political ideals. But all of Li Si's proposals—at least until his last days, when, as we shall see, he was reduced to toadying to unworthy superiors—reflect a consistent and revolutionary view of Qin's mission: to unify the disparate kingdoms and implement a new centralized form of government, while eliminating divergent customs and resisting any policy that might lead to a recrudescence of territorial power.

At some point between 219 and 213 B.C.E., Li Si was promoted to chancellor, and was now one of the two highest-ranking subjects in the empire.[4] In 213, a scholar named Chunyu Yue remonstrated with the First Emperor, repeating the old suggestion that the sons and younger brothers of the Emperor, along with certain meritorious ministers, should be enfeoffed as feudal lords. The First Emperor handed the matter down to Chancellor Li Si, who was even more emphatic in his rejection of this proposal than when he had first discussed the issue eight years earlier. In his later reply, he did not even attempt to refute Chunyu Yue's suggestion, taking it as agreed that such ideas were hopelessly outdated. Instead, Li Si addressed what he took to be the real problem: men like Chunyu Yue took the liberty of criticizing official decrees on the basis of what he calls their "private learning." This is unacceptable, Li Si argues, because in the new unified regime, only the emperor has the authority to determine right and wrong. If "private learning" is not prohibited, "the power of the ruler will decline above and parties will be formed below."

Li Si then recommends that every subject who possesses works of literature, including the canonical *Odes* and *Documents* and the "sayings of the hundred schools," must remand these to the appropriate officials for burning. Anyone who wants to study must take an administrative official as his teacher. The only exceptions to this ordinance are books on medicine, divination, and agriculture; according to one version of the memorial, Li Si allows government-appointed Academicians to retain their copies of canonical texts. The First Emperor, we are told, approved the measure.

This was the notorious "Qin biblioclasm," the event with which Li Si has been most intimately connected in the minds of traditional Chinese literati. Generations of historians have criticized Li Si as an enemy of learning in general and Confucianism in particular. Indeed, he cannot be easily acquitted of these charges. On the other hand, some modern scholars have suggested that the entire account is fabricated or at least exaggerated, because the memorial implies a massive campaign to collect books and burn them, but there is little evidence that any texts were permanently lost. That observation, however, is not in itself compelling: texts were commonly memorized and recited in ancient China, so that even if all written copies were destroyed, they could still be reconstructed afterward (provided that enough people who knew the text by heart were left). In fact, the Han government made a concerted effort some decades later to locate the aged masters of the Qin era and have them recite what they could remember for scribes to record with brush and ink. Moreover, if we are to believe the account that official Academicians were exempt from the ban, then it follows that the canons were never totally abolished in the first place.

Whether or not the "biblioclasm" really took place, it is clear that the proposal is in keeping with Li Si's political views. "Private learning," as Li Si put it, is antithetical to the pretensions of the unified empire, and eradicating all autonomous intellectual life was only the logical conclusion of the reforms that he had been advocating for years. Any institution whose authority did not derive directly from the emperor inherently challenged the foundations of the empire and had to be destroyed. Philosophers and teachers, who routinely appealed to traditions, scriptures, and august precedents, would have constituted a conspicuous example of what Li Si feared most. The Qin Empire was not merely an empire; it was a unified cosmos with a proper cosmology. The ruler of the cosmos, similarly, was not merely an emperor or great king; he was the center of the cosmos, the prime mover of all order and logic. He was God.

In short, Li Si was unable to conceive of a flourishing empire that countenanced free thought, let alone dissent. By imposing its rigid dictates on all aspects of human experience, the empire sowed the seeds of its own destruction. To Americans living in the twenty-first century, it may seem obvious that Li Si's attempts at thought control were to blame for the astonishingly rapid collapse of the Qin dynasty. But it took a long decade of intense bloodletting for the point to become apparent to observers in the third century B.C.E.

Li Si was now at the peak of his power, and Sima Qian includes a picturesque episode in his biography intended to show that the Chancellor himself may have had a premonition that his fortunes were about to turn. At some point after the memorial on the burning of the books, Li Si held a feast at his home to welcome back his son, Li You, who was serving as governor of Sanchuan (a commandery along the Yellow River, east of the capital). It is said that thousands of chariots and horsemen arrived at the gates of his residence as officials from all branches of government came to wish him long life. The Chancellor then quoted his former teacher and compared himself to a useless carriage horse: "Alas, I have heard Xun Qing say: 'Do not let things flourish too greatly.' I wore a commoner's clothes at Shangcai; I was an ordinary subject from the lanes and alleyways. The Emperor did not realize that his nag was inferior, so he raised me to this [position]. No one with a ministerial position occupies a post higher than mine; one can call this the pinnacle of wealth and honor. When things reach their pinnacle, they decline. I do not yet know where my carriage will be halted."

Late in 211 B.C.E., the First Emperor decided to make one of his habitual circuits through his empire, accompanied by Li Si and two other men: Zhao Gao, a eunuch who was superintendent of the Imperial Carriage-House, and Huhai, a young son of the First Emperor. The First Emperor's eldest son, named Fusu, had irritated his father by criticizing him repeatedly for his denigration of Confucius. Consequently, the First Emperor sent Fusu to the camp of General Meng Tian, who was stationed at the frontier. With Fusu far removed from palace politics, it seems that the aging First Emperor began to dote on Huhai as his favorite son.

Nine months into his grand tour, the First Emperor fell deathly ill at a place called Sand Hill. He had a letter written to Fusu, commanding him to come to the capital with Meng Tian's troops and bury his father there. The letter had been sealed but not sent when the First Emperor died. Since no definite heir had been designated, Li Si decided to keep the matter secret, and only he, Zhao Gao, Huhai, and a handful of trusted eunuchs knew that the First Emperor had passed away. They placed the Emperor's cadaver in a "warm-and-cool carriage"—that is, a carriage that could be opened or closed as the climate dictated—and continued to conduct official business from within the closed carriage, as though the Emperor were still alive.[5]

As one of the First Emperor's most intimate associates, Zhao Gao must have known that Huhai was a foolish and malleable lordling. He clandestinely encouraged the young prince to seize the throne for himself, hinting darkly that the empire would not rebel if Fusu were to be assassinated. After obtaining Huhai's consent, Zhao Gao then approached Li Si with his plan, but the latter declined repeatedly to cooperate. Zhao Gao countered by remarking that Fusu trusted only General Meng Tian, his comrade-in-arms, and if Fusu were to succeed the First Emperor, Li Si would surely be replaced as chancellor. Li Si remained unmoved: he and his family had enjoyed great prosperity at the hands of the First Emperor and would remain loyal, come what may. Furthermore, Li Si cited several examples from history showing that such treachery always causes great harm to the state. Zhao Gao importuned Li Si relentlessly, until the latter finally "looked up to Heaven and sighed." With tears streaming down his face, he declared: "Alas, I alone have encountered this chaotic age. Since I cannot bring myself to die, to what shall I entrust my life?" Thereupon he obeyed Zhao Gao.

Modern readers are likely to be puzzled by all of Li Si's sighs and rhetorical questions; and whatever the implicit argument is in "since I cannot bring myself to die, to what shall I entrust my life," it hardly persuades us that his actions were anything but disloyal. This passage probably tells us more about the author, Sima Qian, than it does about Li Si. Having characters gaze up to Heaven at crucial moments in history is a trope that Sima Qian uses on several occasions to suggest that the irresistible will of Heaven lies behind the inscrutable vicissitudes of human life. We must remember that Sima Qian was writing for the Emperor of the Han, a dynasty whose rise would not have been possible without the destruction of the Qin. For a Han audience, the conspiracy at Sand Hill was a matter of historical necessity. Li Si's protestations were gallant but ineffectual: one way or another, Heaven was going to find a way for the plot to unfold. In his gazing up at Heaven, therefore, we are given to understand that Li Si recognized and accepted the role that fate had assigned him.

Huhai's reign as Second Emperor was an unmitigated disaster. A simple power struggle ensued between Li Si and Zhao Gao: both courtiers knew that Huhai was thoroughly incapable of standing on his own, so they competed for the opportunity to rule behind the scenes. This was a contest that Li Si was bound to lose, for Zhao Gao was more adept at manipulating the puerile emperor. With Zhao Gao's encouragement, the Second Emperor ushered in a reign of terror, executing influential men in government and confiscating their estates; although the turmoil amused the Second Emperor, it had the decisive consequence of destroying whatever power base he had at his disposal.

The famous rebellion of Chen She and Wu Guang then erupted in Chu, and with the central government in such disarray, the imperial forces were powerless to quell it. When the rebels arrived at Sanchuan, Li Si's son You, who was still governor of the district, could not stop them from advancing westward toward the imperial capital. Zhao Gao immediately took advantage of this opportunity to accuse Li Si and his son of conniving at the insurrection. Before long, the Chancellor was thrown into prison and brought to trial; once again, he gazed up fecklessly at Heaven, this time comparing himself to various celebrated ministers of antiquity who were wrongly condemned.

The rest of Li Si's biography is devoted to his craven attempts to save his skin. He penned a long and fawning epistle, laying out heavy-handed principles of government that he hoped would meet with the Second Emperor's approval. One of the authorities he cites in this disquisition is Han Fei, the great thinker whose downfall he himself plotted years before; it must have galled him to memorialize his arch rival in this manner, but such was the humiliating stance to which he was reduced. Next he assailed Zhao Gao's integrity, asserting at one point that the eunuch was avaricious because of his lowly origins. (Forensically, this was a doomed approach: after all, Li Si, too, was born a commoner, and his own ambition was of historic proportions.) Then, in a final act of desperation, Li Si wrote a direct plea to the Second Emperor from his jail cell, recounting his great services to the state of Qin and begging for mercy. But Zhao Gao intercepted the letter and refused to show it to the Emperor. In the summer of 208 B.C.E., Li Si and his son were put to death and their clan exterminated.

Sima Qian records Li Si's last words, and they are characteristically disingenuous. On the way to the execution ground, he supposedly turned to his son and said: "I wish that you and I could take our brown dog and go out through the eastern gate of Shangcai to chase the crafty hare. But how could we do that!" This quote has become famous, but, like his repeated perlustrations of Heaven, it is simply an expression of counterfeit pathos. While he was still living in Shangcai, Li Si felt nothing more for the place than an intense desire to leave it, and an innocent bucolic life would hardly have contented him while he was serving in the grimy municipal offices. Or perhaps his last wish is tinged with regret: a life devoted to hunting rabbits might not have been cut short by the executioner's blade.

In the end, regardless of our opinion of him, we must acknowledge that Li Si was the primary architect of early Chinese imperialism, a man whose vision affected the course of history of an entire subcontinent. Most later writers dispraised him as a traitor and an opportunist, but there is no doubt that the imperial institutions of every succeeding dynasty were indebted to Li Si's model of centralized bureaucracy. If, as some scholars affirm, Chinese civilization was a bureaucratic civilization, then a place must be reserved for Li Si as one of the nation's founding fathers.[6]

NOTES

1. There are two complete English translations of the biography: one by Burton Watson, *Records of the Grand Historian: Qin Dynasty*, Hong Kong, 1993, 179–206; and the other by Derk Bodde, *China's First Unifier: A Study of the Ch'in Dynasty as Seen in the Life of Li Ssu (280?–208 B.C.)*, Sinica Leidensia 3 (Leiden: E. J. Brill, 1938), 12–55.

2. Xunzi's collected works (known as the *Xunzi*) contain a fragment of questionable authenticity, in which Li Si argues with his teacher over the reasons for Qin's success. The passage is translated in John Knoblock, *Xunzi: A Translation and Study of the Complete Works*, 3 vols., Stanford, 1988–94, 3:228–29.

3. Sima Qian's chapter on the state of Han records the date as 234; this is possible if we assume that Han Fei departed from Han late in 234 and arrived in Qin early the next year. The matter is discussed further in Bodde, *China's First Unifier*, 62–77.

4. This we can deduce from the fact that he is still mentioned in 219 B.C.E. as a "chamberlain"; the same Wang Wan and one Wei Zhuang (sometimes called Wei Lin) are listed as chancellors in that year. But the sources are clear that Li Si was chancellor by 213. It is commonly, but erroneously, supposed that Li Si was appointed chancellor immediately after the unification in 221; even as eminent a scholar as Michael Loewe, in *A Biographical Dictionary of the Qin, Former Han and Xin Periods (221 B.C.–A.D. 24)*, *Handbuch der Orientalistik*, vol. 4, no. 16: p. 228, Leiden, 2000, makes this mistake. The source of the confusion is probably Li Si's biography in *Records of the Historian*, which implies that he was already chancellor when he objected to Wang Wan's feudalistic proposals, though it is clear from the Annals of the First Emperor that he was then still Commandant of Justice.

5. An ancient bronze model of such a chariot was recently excavated, and it is currently on display in the Shaanxi Provincial Museum in Xi'an.

6. See, for example, Etienne Balazs, *Chinese Civilization and Bureaucracy: Variations on a Theme*, translated by H. M. Wright and edited by Arthur F. Wright, New Haven, 1964.

SUGGESTED READINGS

Bodde, Derk. *China's First Unifier: A Study of the Ch'in Dynasty as Seen in the Life of Li Ssu (280?–208 B.C.)*. Sinica Leidensia 3, Leiden, 1938. This is still the only book-length study of Li Si in English and it includes translations of all the relevant primary texts, though the approach to the sources is somewhat dated.

_____. "The State and Empire of Ch'in." In *The Cambridge History of China*, vol. I: *The Ch'in and Han Empires*, edited by Denis Twitchett and Michael Loewe, 20–102. Cambridge, England, 1986.

Durrant, Stephen. "Ssu-ma Ch'ien's Portrayal of the First Emperor." In *Imperial Rulership and Cultural Change in Traditional China*, edited by Frederick P. Brandauer and Chun-chieh Huang, 28–50, Seattle, 1994. This is an incisive study of Sima Qian's treatment of the First Emperor and Qin imperial institutions, with passing references to Li Si.

Hsiao, Kung-chuan. *A History of Chinese Political Thought*, vol. 1: *From the Beginnings to the Sixth Century A.D.*, translated by F. W. Mote. Princeton Library of Asian Translations. Princeton, 1979. This standard work contains a section on Li Si's political philosophy on pages 434–46.

CHAPTER 3

Lives and Times of the Political Public at the End of the Han

Howard L. Goodman

Throughout Chinese history, families have been the basic unit of society. During the Han dynasty, as the imperial order forged at the beginning of the second century B.C.E. stabilized, a fundamental shift took place in Chinese political culture, in which a group of great aristocratic families emerged as the dominant elite of the empire, replacing the military character of earlier ruling groups. Although the imperial polity underwent considerable flux over the next few centuries, the social order that developed during the Han remained basically intact through the middle years of the Tang dynasty (617–907 C.E.).

At the end of the Han and into the ensuing Three Kingdoms period (220–265 C.E.), one such great family was the Cao. Howard Goodman, an independent scholar in Seattle, uses the Cao family to lead us into the aristocratic world of the third century, introducing two other important clans and a number of additional individuals to fill out his story. This is a collective biography of some of the major players in a time of great drama and intense human struggles. The Three Kingdoms has remained a period of fascination for later Chinese generations, and many myths and legends as well as works of popular fiction and theater have grown out of it. Here Goodman presents a solid historical narrative that is just as exciting and action filled as any literary rendition.

Our modern public life is filled with wild and often discordant phenomena; anti-World Trade Organization protests, pundits and spin doctors, gangster-chic television shows and rap music, prophecy and divination, terrorism and power grabs. We look a lot like second- and third-century China, and the fables and romances that described a time of intense fighting and bandits of bizarre charisma, of omens and dreams, and the loss of a political center. It pays to keep this in mind, although it is wrong to explain early China as parallel historically to such a vastly different culture as ours. It was not even a parallel to Mediterranean antiquity. Many students first attracted to early Western history have instinctive expectations, something like "icons" that reflect certain mysteries they hope to unlock—the hierarchies of Egyptian temple culture or the feudal and theological bonds important at medieval courts. Those expectations must be trained up by working with reconstructions built on small, accessible facts and realities. Was a village an entrepôt (a trading site) on a long-distance route? Were most inhabitants simply artisans working for a small dominant group? What were they making? Was there turmoil there, a coalescing movement? From whom did people take political cues or leadership?

Our aim here is to peer briefly into the lives and times of families in China between about 190 and 260 C.E. Families were the nexus of leadership in their home locales and even nationally, and provided office-holders for the court bureaucracy. Many provided military support or matériel for a preferred overlord, dozens of whom existed in all regions of China. Members of families traveled, witnessed turmoil, and felt the loss of the political center or of their own careers. Moreover, their elders handed down different sorts of education and skills, such as music, classical texts, traditional divination, court ritual, and religious mysteries.

KEYS TO THE PERIOD

The period known as the Three Kingdoms, with the beginning of the Period of Division, starts at the time of the collapse of the Han dynasty, encompassing roughly the years from the 180s C.E. to 220 C.E., but marked violently in the year 190 with the burning of the Han capital by a war-lord who could not hold power for long. The period continues to the point at which Chinese courts and boundaries had completely shifted and the large political–economic sphere that the Han once controlled was split up by non-Chinese invaders—that is, to about the middle of the fourth century. It is crucial to explain, first off, that for this specific period we are not blessed with archaeological overviews (except for a small number of sites of crumbling city walls and several tomb graphics and some tomb goods), nor with textual ones: we have no near-contemporary syntheses of social and political developments. Thus, for trade, markets, taxation, demography, and whatever tenets may have been espoused by popular rebel movements, we have only patchy accounts and anecdotes.

Although the material and court-archival sources are poor, several types of textual source material do exist that have been used for centuries. They are the accounts and anecdotes just mentioned: writings of educated, highly literate members of the elite, or as I prefer to call them, the "political public." Such writings were preserved through court-established compendia and private activity. These were continually retranscribed, commented on, and then printed and disseminated and studied even more thoroughly when printing and the examination system became more fully developed much later. Some of these are the so-called standard histories that recorded edicts, lives of court and royal personages, and political actions. Other textual sources are the poems, essays, and belles lettres that eventually entered well-known compendia; a few of the early-dated texts that were later anthologized as sacred texts of Daoism and Buddhism; and, finally, inscriptions originally carved on tomb walls and free-standing monuments. Inscriptions usually commemorated a deceased person, a religious site, a court policy, or a mythic hero of deep antiquity or relative contemporaneity. These inscriptions were copied and widely studied over centuries, even when the original site and inscription had long been erased.

The veracity of the textual sources has been subjected to severe criticism in China (particularly in the standard histories), or too little utilized (the inscriptions and the tracts of Daoism and Buddhism). But many of such criticisms were overreactions and rooted in old controversies about political rightness and the "mandate of heaven" in the post–Han era, or the critics simply disdained disturbing aspects of that political and popular culture. Since the late nineteenth century, however, we have begun to give careful credence to texts relating family situations and personal biography, accounts of deeds and battles, memos to courts, and inscribed memorials. We have begun to utilize facts and patterns of fact that either have no potential for falsity or are otherwise corroborated (by edicts, court actions, appointments, battles, dates, and the like). Some historians believe, correctly in my opinion, that we should not throw out texts of speeches or of private affairs merely because they narrate unusual bravado or charisma, or strange events and practices like divination, dream prophecies, and communities of Dao-worshipers. Some members of the political public in early China wrote only for their families and associates; some wrote for social and court prestige. But most seem to have treated anecdote and narrative seriously—as evidences of history. They did not usually invent the acts of bravado, prophecy, or religious rebellion, although some embellished and smoothed out the flow because of the values of the genre in which they worked. We must, therefore, accept that in a time of intense political stress people took stunning risks and held unusual loyalties. We recognize that, as educated and scholarly people, they spoke with flair about their family and friends and wrote down their ideas, which would become anthologized. We must also place this in another, larger, cultural context: China's ancient modes of religious, mortuary, and "nonrational" expression were bursting out of traditional, Confucianist bonds in this period and adopting genres and pathways that would remain strong in China until modern times.

Chinese historians have strongly characterized the period and created the sort of iconic notions we considered earlier. First, the period under consideration is thought to have been one of unique political and martial bravery and romance: as the power of the Han central court collapsed, dynasty-forming overlord families engaged in schemes and strategies that filled the imagination and inspired centuries of poetry, image, and drama. The most famous is a long cycle called *Romance of the Three Kingdoms*. At the basic level, all the stories depend on reliable facts about the various early courts and schemers. But these were puffed up and stylized, beginning in the Tang and Song eras and culminating in sixteenth- and seventeenth-century fiction that is as important to the Chinese as our own Knights of the Round Table. Some of the heroes were regicides; some, burners of capital cities; and some, valiant and godlike. These are examples of certain ideas and actions that disturbed later historians, who, fortunately, were not also the playwrights and dramatists.

Second, Chinese historians have mourned, above all, the political "loss": any possibility for moral leadership from a dynastic house with a "mandate of heaven" to lead the larger Chinese polity was weakened by a succession of regimes that held only small areas and lacked the ability and luck to regain the whole polity. The fact is that, by the early fourth century, the sites of the old Han court (at first at Chang'an in the west and then shifted to the more central Loyang) were taken over by invading non-Chinese from both the northwest and northeast, who set up their own dynasties, and the culture of the northern court elite moved south of the Yangtze River on a large scale. Chinese historians have disagreed even down to modern times as to which, if any, of the successor courts (after the 190s) may have held the mandate, even indirectly or in small part, thus contributing to a feeling of permanent tragedy.

Third, but by no means least, the Three Kingdoms and the beginning of the Period of Division were a time that Chinese historians have seen as a flowering of literary and philosophical interest in "mystery"— a specific Chinese term with several meanings, but more important to us as a general description. It is not to be thought of precisely as mysticism—that is, forces that call to the human sensibility and that come from spirits, the dead, or secret teachings, but it touched on that. It was a mixture. It had to do with remnants of both Daoist religious communities and Daoist notions that were being revived in new textual editions of pre-Han writings, some of which had previously been poorly understood and transmitted. Also, "mystery" figured in passionate orations that arose in times of power struggles. Such struggles usually engendered talk of legitimacy, and seekers of legitimacy used traditional Chinese practices like divination, omens, and cryptic messages that many felt came from China's most ancient founding sages and that were revealed in spurious "classical" texts. Outside this specific political context, many writers took up "mysteries" in terms of the classics, court ritual, Daoist and other kinds of transcendent truth—or even afterlife divinations and ghosts. During this period, we also see a "spin" just beginning, with the appearance of Buddhist translators. The process began to reflect itself in otherwise Confucian literary arenas beginning around the fourth century, so it will not be treated here.

EXAMPLES OF LEADING FAMILIES AND THE POLITICAL PUBLIC

It is impossible to convey here the large picture of battles for political control, court policies and intrigues, and the economic patterns of locales. In fact, as already mentioned, such a reliable summary, especially for economic and material culture, is hard to develop for this period. Instead, we can learn something about the careers and intellectual choices of several members of well-known families. Families and associations (both private and official) in this era in China were the principal means by which influence and leadership were obtained.

First we look at the new dynast, Cao Pi, proclaimed in 220 C.E. as the first emperor of the Wei dynasty, which took power from the Han (although holding only militarily the old central–north and northwest), and his position within his famous family of military men, and his relations with other men of influence. We shall be asking the question: how did a new emperor deal with experts, scholars, generals, and various local leaders, many of whose families had been holding state offices under the Han for generations? Did they exert political pressure on him, and if so, how was that done, especially in the context of groups (to be seen in some sense as blocs) and family connections?

After Cao Pi, we consider two other men and their families and touch on still others. The two families are the Wangs of Donghai in the northeast and the Yus of Guiji (southeast coastal China, the modern Shanghai area). We see connections among them, but those families in no way represented their own bloc. In fact, the Yus represent a rather isolatable southern experience, although they maintained numerous contacts with the north. We see careers that were rising at the end of the Han and the beginning of Cao Pi's new dynasty. But we see also changes in the way young men from these families were to find their mark in a new China.

THE STRUCTURE OF SOCIETY

In simple terms, China was then a three-level society, similar to Chinese society of previous centuries. The imperial family (1), in principle, the controller of all lands, offices, and state wealth, was at the top. The emperor often shared wealth, land, and privileges with the princes of the blood, princesses, and families of consorts, and delegated quite a bit of authority to palace eunuchs. In practice, though, attempts by the emperor (or privileged parties) to exercise total control were limited by (2) the state's administrative officials and their staffs, who represented the second level. This level contained an extremely small portion of all households in China, but it had achieved a legally recognized status. Males received state salaries and tenure, as well as various rewards, when placed in office. They had exemptions from tax, corvée (labor and quasi-military conscriptions), and various criminal punishments. The third stratum of society (3), enormous in comparison, consisted of all nonofficial households—farming, trading, military, and artisan, whose members occasionally gained lower-level offices and moved into the second level.

Among viable families at that level, there were gradations: great clans, minor clans from the outlying provinces, and low-born families from farming, trading, or military backgrounds. During this period many men had entered into officialdom from relatively low origins. Their access was in part due to the court's emphasis, accelerating in the last part of the Han, on its nonmilitary functionaries—men from respectable backgrounds who were scholiasts, writers, and experts in documents, ritual, and ceremony. This shift had opened up offices to those who could demonstrate basic literacy and reasonable connections. Naturally, the military wings of the state remained, but this civilian aspect grew tremendously.

The political public was not an actual term for a social phenomenon or group like the terms "officials" or nonofficial "*min*" (the farming and toiling populace). I use it as a convenience only, because we need to have a sense of just who in China was party to or at least conversant with the decisions and events of the court, or with influential officials outside the court. That public would have consisted of all of level 1 (but, in 189, thousands of court eunuchs and their staff were murdered and eliminated completely as a political group); probably 75 percent of level 2, including many low-ranked officials (and retired or secluded teachers, military men, writers, and the like) who did not hold offices but remained in locales; and, last, a small number of artisans, merchants, and the rest, especially those at or near the court itself or serving the interests of important households in the provinces. The political public made up only a small percentage of China's population, probably no more than 5 to

10 percent. I estimate that in modern U.S. society, probably 70 to 80 percent of the adult population takes part in the political culture in some way (even passively), and of that group, maybe half take matters of policy and taxation seriously, at least at the local level, and also vote. Ours is quite an enormous political public.

The Han dynasty's methods of selecting and appointing civil officers had grown ineffective by the 160s and 170s. Local leaders, acting independently of the Han court, began recommending young men to official posts, thus building up power bases of their own. Their sons were educated, learned the classics, and served as loyal assistants to private teachers or local officials. Increasingly, court appointments to provincial administration became powerful tools for families, especially as court service became dangerous. In the 160s, many well-known officials opposed the Eastern Han emperor Lingdi (and the eunuch bloc that controlled him) and were forced violently to leave service at the capital. This exclusion created a long-lasting hostility.

It is in this context that the post–Han period witnessed the beginning of an aristocracy of officialdom that would reach full flower by the Sui–Tang period. By about 223, under Cao Pi's new Wei dynasty, the independent style of nomination to office became co-opted as a court policy, first in name and then more functionally beginning in 250, under the dynasty that succeeded the Wei, the Sima family's Jin dynasty. Sons of high officials could now regularly expect midrank appointments to the court as their first positions. It was a way for the dynasty to share power and once again open up the family-held routes to high office that they had developed early in the Han but later lost.

Families of this type helped one another and by doing so extended their viability. Those in the same or neighboring commanderies frequently traded teaching duties, adopted offspring if a family's condition deteriorated, and, most important, intermarried. Yingchuan is a primary example of local networks. Three influential families there were the Xuns, Zhongs, and Chens. The Xuns had estates and raised troops in support of Cao Pi's famous and active father Cao Cao. Xun You brought Zhong You and his own relative Xun Yu into Cao Cao's camp. Zhong women married Xun men, and so forth. This is merely an example of webs of private and court interaction that grew in part from shared provincial roots.

For nonofficials, unfortunately we have few traditional or newly discovered texts to describe their management of homes and social networks. We do know, though, that the central government and local leaders spent considerable energy in organizing the labors of local and itinerant artisans, producers, and fighting men. Powerful officials developed lands and estates in agricultural and urban areas. Often, the personnel of these landed estates would number in the many thousands, including soldiers and farming families who sought haven. Cao Cao (as an example) used the services of such soldiers, treating them officially as military households to be mustered into service when situations required it. Anecdotes in the standard sources do show that troops were often treated as a personal constituency. Furthermore, a well-known economic policy of the Han court, referred to as "garrison farms," was reimplemented in the 180s through the 210s by the overlords who fought for control. Cao Cao and others established large forces of soldiers and others on war-ravaged lands and, in many cases, surrendered non-Chinese warriors or Chinese rebels were placed there under supervision.

THE POLITICAL SETTING

During the reigns of Han emperors Huandi (r. 147–167) and Lingdi (r. 168–189), three political groups at the capital vied with each other—the eunuchs, who acted as handlers of emperors and accrued much power; the empresses and their families, who frequently maintained military control; and, finally, leading officialdom, whose members attempted to reform the throne and control appointments to offices. Great numbers of members of the landed local families had been expelled from the capital and persecuted during Lingdi's reign. It was a season of revolts in the provinces, particularly the several-years-long Daoist-inspired Yellow Turban peasant rebellion. As these increased in the 180s, the throne recalled able officials in hopes of their guiding a large-scale effort to defeat the Turbans and restore a functioning central government. Another cycle of rebellion began in Liangzhou in the far west; it was rooted in the court's previous attempts to pacify the so-called Qiang and Di non-Chinese peoples. The Han court was no longer effective, and the most powerful of court-appointed generals held on to their territories and developed local courts in order to rule independently. In 190, Loyang, the national capital situated in the Honan commandery, was looted and burned by the most fractious and dangerous of these generals, and the Han court was removed briefly to Chang'an, while other overlords plotted to defeat this general. Central bureaucratic control by the Han house was effectively ended.

From this came a geographic separation of China into the Three Kingdoms (Sanguo). Cao Cao established a foothold in the Central Plain by the 190s, gaining allies and troops as he fought the Turbans and others. Through a confusing series of events, he also gained control of the boy-emperor Han Xiandi, and in 196 set him up in a temporary national capital in Xu, near Loyang. In the Central South about 190, Liu Biao

(d. 208) established a court and a military presence at Xiangyang that collapsed with his death. In the southeast, the Sun family led first by Sun Ce and his younger brother Sun Quan, attacking and co-opting landed gentry, began rule as the Kingdom of Wu. By about 214, Liu Bei (161–223) established a court in western China, an area strong in agriculture and textile and lacquer products. But Liu's Shu kingdom faced a threat from Zhang Lu's "Five-Peck" (or Celestial Master) Daoists, a religious and military organization that ruled Hanzhong commandery in the northeast corner of Shu (the old name for what is mostly Sichuan) until 216.

CAO PI'S EMERGENCE AS EMPEROR
AND A NATIONAL STYLE

Cao Pi's father, Cao Cao, was one of the new heroes. His life became the stuff of legend even in his own day and was the subject of both nasty screeds and glowing narratives. It is still expected of Chinese students that they know something about him. But I want to introduce post-Han lives and times through the son, who became emperor of the Wei dynasty in 220, taking the throne from the last Eastern Han emperor.

It is important to bear in mind that in Cao Pi we have someone broadly similar to others to be discussed below—in terms of local and court power, education, cultural sensibility, and intellectual mood. But in terms of political pressures he was different. He was trained to compete even with family members. The Caos led troops in fierce campaigns all over China for more than forty years before Cao Pi's coronation. Cao Pi's immediate family branch had been at the center of the Eastern Han court since about 185, but especially so since 196 when Cao Cao had become de facto ruler of China, standing in place of the submissive Eastern Han boy-emperor. One must bear in mind, too, that the Cao family was of low origin, as descended from an adopted son of a court eunuch (an origin usually despised by leading families). Furthermore, in the family's early years, marriage links had not been made to old-line families of scholar–officials. Much of the opposition to the Caos came from families who resented these realities.

Cao Pi (187–226) was the son of Cao Cao (then about thirty-two years old) by his consort Bian, herself once a singing girl. Cao Cao at the time of his son's birth was engaged in what would be a five- or six-year campaign against antidynastic rebels in the Central Plain and the northwest. Cao Pi had twenty-five brothers (three full brothers by Bian, and twenty-two half-brothers). Only his full-brother Zhi became well known in history, particularly as a writer. A half-brother, Gan, as well as several cousin–adoptees, constituted a circle of close siblings in addition to Zhi.

When Pi was about seventeen he took as his own consort the Lady Zhen, who had been the consort of one of Cao Cao's northern military rivals, but was found by Cao Pi in pitiful circumstances when his father conquered them at their stronghold in Ye in 204.

Cao Pi's composition on literature titled "Dianlun" (written about 217) claims, "I learned archery at five and at six I mastered it; and they also taught me riding. At eight I was able to shoot from horseback." Although such items are standard in early-Chinese biography, we do not have to rule out the claims: he probably did learn how to ride and shoot when he was a boy. But literary activities were just as important. He and his brothers were ordered by Cao Cao to honor a certain man as their scholarly master, but the latter leaves no trace in the records in a time of many famous scholars who wrote essays and had dozens or hundreds of loyal students. Cao Pi went on to write about belles lettres, sponsor literary activity, and compose his own verses, as his father had done. Was he, then, a typical young man of the educated political public? What in fact were his influences and his motives as a leader?

We know that his father, besides his military skill, was actively interested in literature and ideas and had made sure to surround himself with famous writers and experts, men such as Kong Rong, Zhong You, Wang Lang, Xun Yu, and Wang Can, among others. Kong Rong had been a famous man of letters for decades whom Cao Cao eventually turned against; Zhong You, not only a famous writer and calligrapher, was also an important Cao general; Wang Can was a poet, an expert in music and official ceremonies, and an aide-de-camp on Cao Cao's campaigns. In 208, Cao Cao defeated Liu Biao in the south and as a consequence took over Liu's college of famous ritualists and scholars. Cao Cao sponsored poetry, music, ritual experts, and even Daoist-style "magicians"; and Cao Cao and Cao Zhi in particular wrote poetry and made numerous comments on philosophy and letters. They were not out of the mainstream, even if relatively less cultured in terms of the educational and scholarly concerns of other leading families. Moreover, ideas and orations were essential to any debate about legitimacy, about "heaven's mandate" to succeed the Han.

It is easy to deduce that Cao Pi's learning derived from such great men personally (he once issued a directive to reward anyone submitting examples of Kong Rong's writing), or directly from his father. Yet, none of the Caos is known to have completed what in China was considered a whole course in the Confucian classics; none made a statement or a reputation as participant in certain debates about the classics (for example, the controversy over New Text and Old Text interpretations); none established himself in a scholarly lineage with a famous teacher.

Early in his official career Cao Pi was nominated as a *maocai*, a type of official-in-waiting, but he could not accept it because of a controversy surrounding his father's need to display impartiality. In 207 he was appointed to a low-rank post by his father and given a higher quasi-military office in 211—that of General of the Gentlemen of Household for All Purposes. In this office he may have served only nominally in a military capacity, using the post instead to form a prototype of an heir apparent's consultative staff. There were no mid- or high-ranked civilian court posts in Cao Pi's career, unlike the other men we study whose families held resources and culture, intermarried, and maintained loyalties to ensure that their sons entered a long career of civilian posts, aimed at receiving (usually at about age thirty or so) the most powerful ones at court, or posts as governors and prefects in important provinces.

Before 220, Cao Pi seems not to have been a troop leader. It may be that he was not considered skilled enough, or, before about 210, old enough. We can only guess at the reason for it. He was dissuaded from "going out in person to punish [allies of the rebels Tian Ying and Su Bo]." Later, as emperor in 222, Cao Pi sent troops on an eastern campaign (against Wu), yet apparently did not go with them. In the winter of 222–23 he campaigned southward from Xu, stopping at Wan, in south-central China (Runan commandery). But the next month he issued an edict from Wan deploring the numbers of war dead, and expressing his "grief in mourning [for Cao Cao, who had recently died]." He then had erected a "platform to commemorate the southern campaign." On a later campaign, he stopped for ceremonies at the Xu palaces and "personally commanded a war-junk for the benefit of the navy" and gave large-scale pardons.

Here is a pattern. It was common in early China for military campaigns to be imbued with rituals, and Cao Pi seems to have perfected the art of staging them. In midsummer 220, he directed the traditional *huagai* ritual at the Eastern Suburb site in Loyang, which he continued with a tour, feasting in his home area of Qiao and dispensing mortuary gifts to veterans' families. All of this suggests that his forte was in the public rituals related to the military more than in leading troops into battle.

In fact, Cao Cao initially may have preferred Cao Zhi as his heir apparent because the latter cultivated loyal friends among the most able generals and widely proclaimed his own martial zeal. This is seen in the incident at the Major's Gate (dated perhaps to 217). Cao Cao tested his two sons by ordering each to go out of the city of Ye through the appropriate military gates but secretly had the gates barred beforehand. Zhi fought his way through, but Pi pulled up short and returned. Cao Cao later used Zhi's abuse of power in that incident, and some other matters, in order to reject him as his successor. The incident seems to have been a test of proper obedience to military regulations rather than of military brashness.

Cao Pi's life up to 220 (the year Cao Cao died and Cao Pi took the throne) was marked by associations with two leading families in particular—the Xiahous and Simas. The Xiahous were from the same locale as the Caos. Three of their numbers were allied with Cao Cao as generals in important campaigns, and Cao Pi was reported as having been close with two of them. The Simas were a leading family from Henei commandery (north of Yingchuan). We examine this latter relationship, because it shows that families in the national military spotlight could act together in political situations while still harboring deep tensions among themselves, and with Sima Yi (179–251), we see a career of military campaigns and civilian offices that differed from that of Cao Pi.

Sima Yi's first official post was as a clerk in Cao Cao's armies, probably between about 205 and 208, while Cao Pi was a similarly placed clerk. Around 214, Sima was promoted to Cao Pi's personal staff after Cao Cao had been made duke of Wei. When Cao Pi became king of Wei in 220, he was promoted and ennobled. Up to this point, it is important to point out that Sima had received about nine civilian posts appropriate to a man of his station, and after 220 he received even higher ones (including military titles). He was raised to noble rank, and increases were made in the number of income generating farm households assigned to him. In 226, the dying Cao Pi made him regent along with two Cao-family generals. From there on, Sima Yi exerted increasing pressure on the Cao-family rulers of the Wei dynasty, finally vanquishing them and toppling the regime. Sima Yi's life is documented with numerous specifics relating to his military leadership and skill. He accompanied troops and implemented strategy and techniques. He saw action in, for example, Ye, Xu, Wan, Liaodong in the far northeast, Shouchun, and Ch'angan. He had helped Cao Cao in one of the anti–Zhang Lu campaigns, and was a naval tactician and engineer.

The locales of Honei, Yingchuan (Cao Pi and Sima Yi both had ancestors in the office of the Yingchuan Grand Commandant), and Qiao wove the Caos, Xiahous, and Simas together, and we saw that Sima Yi and Cao Pi likely served together on Cao Cao's staff. But Sima Yi's career subsided for a while. In fact, in 214, Sima Yi was subordinate to Cao Pi at court, although older and in line for higher positions. As we shall see below, Sima Yi did not shirk from rising up to give stern counsel the moment Cao Pi considered establishing a new dynasty. The Xiahous, ever more loyal, extended a traditional and expected form of gesture—as one of many military signers of a pro-Wei document that was carved on a stone marker and set up as an official commemoration.

Cao Pi's relationships and networks with the many dozens of families, the important political public to whom the Caos had to turn for advice and support, seem to have been few before his father's death. In fact, the most powerful impact he had upon them then was negative, however unavoidable from the point of view of the Cao family. In 219 a plot to overturn Cao Cao was exposed: the plotters had planned to take power in Ye, but Cao Cao crushed them peremptorily. He then had Cao Pi order numerous executions, seeking out even those associated only by implication. The victims included sons of beloved writers and court figures. One family hit hard was that of Wang Can (one of the writers mentioned above). Wang had died in 217, but his two sons were executed in the purge. Soon afterward, Cao Pi, now fully entrenched as successor to his father, made apologies and issued tokens of appreciation to some of the more eminent of the survivors, and he continued to make such gestures for years. This was astute politics, and fit Cao Pi's aspirations to lead a literary court and to gain the graces of the leading families.

I have mentioned something about the sources for this period. One of the most effective and convincing ways to reconstruct the lives and times of the early-Chinese political public is to give full context for some anecdotes and speeches in order to get a handle on its members' intellectual positions and moods. This works well in the case of Cao Pi.

The several months preceding enthronement constituted an influential procedure that may be called the legitimation and coronation counsel of 220-21. The earliest sources emphasize the details given at this stage to ceremonies, the participation of groups of partisans as well as single representatives of leading families, and the thousands of expectant onlookers. Cao Pi elongated this counsel brilliantly in order to firm up his overall legitimacy; he employed both time-tested and new methods of arguing his mandate. He brought close dozens of men from the high tier of the political public, many of whom sought rewards of high office or access. Clearly Cao Pi, although having proven himself an able military administrator, needed more than military awe and reliance on loyal generals. He needed ideas as well, and in the light of this, leading families were able to push him in various directions. In what follows, I draw on several significant episodes in the long process, to demonstrate Cao Pi's attitudes toward important cultural values, his handling of potentially nonaligned forces in his domain, and his ability to capture the spirit of the moment through both revered Confucian classics and new texts with new ideas.

CAO PI EMERGES FROM THE CROWD

The Celestial Master Daoists from Sichuan

Only in recent decades has any historian drawn attention to certain facts concerning the role of the Daoist rebel movement of Sichuan that lay behind what we know of Cao Pi's legitimation counsel. Through such work we learn that the Celestial Masters, led until 216 by Zhang Lu in the hills of northern Sichuan, in the Hanzhong commandery, formed a large and cohesive group that moved en masse after Cao Cao defeated them; they were considered a constituency by Cao Cao and Cao Pi, nevertheless, and remained numerous and had representatives at Cao Pi's new court. Their influence increased under the reign of Cao Pi's son (Cao Jui r. 226–239). The earliest sources in fact gave indications that Cao Cao and Zhang Lu began to achieve a curious détente toward the end of the military campaign in 215–16, and this détente was quickly puffed up into another fable of bizarre alliance and mysterious loyalties. It was made all the more mysterious because of Zhang's role as leader of a Daoist community. Therefore, when, during the counsel, Cao Pi was approached by a member of that defeated (and now protected) community with an omen about his legitimacy, historians coming after the fifth century (when the written speeches from this counsel were first anthologized) passed it by. It was to them merely another example of a bothersome "mystery."

Yet what occurred has the earmarks of real political history containing verifiable episodes. The men who approached Cao Pi were trying to legitimize not only Cao Pi but also their own leadership, so that their group could survive. They presented an oracle that had once circulated in Sichuan. The gist of it was that people of refined intelligence (those who handled omens of this sort) realized that Cao Cao never had heaven's mandate; it was Cao Pi's all along. Furthermore, Zhang Lu had heard about the omen and became enraged when his advisers urged him to surrender to Cao Cao's larger enemy in Sichuan, Liu Bei, and he made disparaging remarks about Cao Pi. The omen purported to draw its authority from a writing in the genre of political oracle-texts that had proved so important and effective when the Western Han fell and the Eastern Han arose two centuries before.

It was now clear, in 220, that oracle-texts had returned, and Cao Pi would be forced to deal with them. He could choose to dispense with them and toss the hoped-for influence of these Daoists out of court, or have the oracle debated by stolid Confucian scholars in his entourage, or accept it happily. He chose the last, but employed a flexible solution. The primary political benefit was that such omens were popularly credible; and the omen showed both his father (who had died only six or seven months previously) and his father's strange new ally Zhang Lu (who had died of natural causes among his followers in about 217) in a bad light. This gave him the nod of legitimacy.

Cao Pi's speech, accepting the role of the Celestial Masters, at one point stated: "How can I, a man of meek power [the traditional, and nuanced Chinese term *de*, which referred to charisma and human integrity, as much as political strength], have put forward this [revelation]? I would not dare to presume. In this, truly the former king's [that is, Cao Cao's] utmost *de* has communicated with spirit-intelligence; it is definitely not the work of a mortal."[1]

The speech capped the opening scenario of the counsel and it was politically astute. Cao Pi knew that he had flung open the door for the mysteries of divination, oracle-taking, omens, and the like. He stated his belief that such things were real: they were the work of spirits, not mere living men like himself. But he went further, placing his father, recently buried and being mourned, already in the role of an ancient sage, the kind of person normally thought to issue such omens in the form of mysterious appendices to the Confucian classics. Cao Pi thus had many aspects of this going his way: the Daoists, their omen, and his father's still appealing charisma.

At the same time, he allowed the Celestial Masters to continue intact, although a strong leader would not arise among them. Cao Cao had rewarded some of them after Zhang Lu's death, and those rewards—a place for their minions to reside, noble titles, placement of various Zhang offspring at the Cao court, sometimes as consorts—were continued and increased. Cao Pi effectively co-opted them. And by showing mourning–respect, albeit in an almost unheard-of context (one's father instantly becoming a myth–sage), Cao Pi would not offend the many followers who still held loyalty to Cao Cao, or to other Caos whom they might have preferred as the new emperor.

Oracles vs. Philosophy

A major aspect of the counsel was, at this point, and from the view of the Confucian scholars present, to make sure that the mystery texts and divinities would not be abused. They were to remain and could be interpreted favorably given a chance: they were known entities. But Cao Pi would have to be hemmed in, lest he gain too much leverage from such revelatory sources, instead of the more normative policy stances.

For several weeks, eight local leaders played a large role, issuing appeals and oratories to Cao Pi, who still simply toyed with the notion of beginning the abdication ceremonies, something people expected and were growing anxious over. Four of these men were originally from the south, with various former ties to the southern overlords whom the Caos had battled for years. One in fact had been considered by the Caos as marginally loyal: his older brother acted against his own overlord Liu Biao in Nanyang years ago, the family had associations with the Simas, and the younger brother was one of those executed by Cao Pi in 219 during the purge of the anti-Cao faction, mentioned above. This marks an important point—that Cao Pi wanted marginal loyalists in his midst, so he could co-opt them and keep them under observation. The four northerners had particularly strong ties to Yingchuan, that important political region.

What is unusual about this group is that their task seems to have been to verify and authorize oracles—and nothing more. Most had solid reputations as troop commanders, often at some time or other working loyally with the Caos. The northerners in particular were well-known as scholars: one was an old Yingchuan eminence with deep knowledge of the classics, the law code, and even court astronomy; and another was a specialist in teaching the classics. Nearly all these core advisers, interestingly enough, were experts in various aspects of court ritual involving transfer of power: the required omens, writs, seals, and other objects or ceremonies.

This is not the place to walk through their arguments, which are difficult and lengthy. We need only know that they presented no appeals to Cao Pi based on the Confucian classics and the philosophical points made therein that concern rulership, political ethics, and the mandate commonly thought to derive from heaven (that is, China's ancient sages). They simply defended the mysteries—presenting a whole packet of oracle-texts, one being the same source that the Daoists had cited—by calling in an oracle-text expert who clarified all their points. They showed the public that Cao Pi was the recipient of the mandate, purely on technical grounds.

As in the previous weeks, Cao Pi rose to this occasion to good effect. He accepted their conclusion (hardly unexpected), yet used the Confucian classics in speeches of his own to make his acceptance extremely indirect and passive. He continued to call himself unworthy of such anointment. Again, he was having it both ways politically.

> In former times Zhou Wen-[wang] divided the world into three, but possessed two, thereby honoring Yin [i.e., the ancient Zhou knew how to share with those whom they defeated]. Confucius admired his great virtue. Gong Dan [Zhougong] examined the histories of emperors and listened to opinions everywhere, and ultimately "restored [the government of the] brilliant sovereign to the child.". . . Although my own virtue does not reach the level of these two sages, can I dare to forget the meaning of [the lines in the

Shi (the classic *Book of Odes*) that refer to]: "The high hill [is looked up to]/ The great road [is easily to be traveled on]." Now, since the legends of Yao, Shun, and Yu all have to do with sagely substance and resplendent virtue, then I may [in parallel] blend with the numinous spirits above and take care of the myriad surnames [that is, the people] below, channeling and fitting [the ancient situation] with that of the present day. But at present my virtue is of the weakest sort and my [conduct as] a man is inferior.

I have experienced [this] fortuitous moment, lucky enough to have followed upon the unfinished work of the former king [Cao Cao]. . . . [When] I go down [that is, die] and confront the former king [in the underworld], I shall have staved off harsh upbraiding. . . . My heart is twittering and my hands are numb [upon listening to the long speeches verifying the oracle-texts]. When I write, I cannot form the graphs; in speaking, I cannot send out my heart's [intentions]. In a moment free of duties I have composed a poem:

"Death and disorder," "reaching far" past bounds,
Blanched bones jumbled myriad *li* around.
"Mourn, mourn": "the little people" have no help.
It is I who'll aid the times, set [affairs] without flaw;
"Restore brilliance to the son," [only then] to withdraw.[2]

Cao Pi's response leverages one Confucian classic in particular, the *Book of Odes*. The first reference to it ("The high hill") refers to the need to press on at difficult tasks in order to gain rewards later on. Most important of all, it was well known (as all lines of the Confucian classics were) and used by Cao Cao on occasion and Cao Pi in other contexts. The small poem that Cao Pi offers at the close here is based heavily on that same classic and keys his public into Cao Pi's own feeling about having risen out of a rather gnarly family ("death and disorder" was from a poem about brotherly conflict, and "reaching far" from one that touches on following in one's father's footsteps). The poem also referred to the *Book of Documents*, which at one point describes the way in which Zhougong placed his nephew, "the restored son," into power. In sum, Cao Pi's stylized humility starts with further expressions of mourning and the hope to see his father in the next world and not be upbraided, and ends with the notion that, like Zhougong who offered up the "son," so, too, would he act as merely that kind of "son," who derives his position from his more able elders.

We last look into the mind of a third-century emperor to examine a challenge given him: Confucian ethics were far more important for a potential dynast than the disturbingly mechanical oracular slogans. The challenge came from a group of men that included Sima Yi:

We subjects have heard that when the era of Yao went into decline the mandate of heaven was then to be found in Shun. When Shun's era declined the mandate was to be found in Yu of Xia. If this is the case, then the numinous power of heaven and earth, the cycles of calendar reckoning, and the tallies concerning dismissing and appointing [rulers] depend solely on virtue. In this regard, Confucius has said: "The phoenix does not come; the river gives forth no chart. It is all over with me!"[3]

The argument, then, is that virtue (again, *de*) is the force that produced the oracles under discussion, thus it is not a mechanism but a philosophical point to be understood. They refer to Confucius (via the *Analects*), who spoke about the fact that heaven-sent tallies judged the existence or lack of moral worth. And when a virtuous man was not available, tallies would indicate that by their silence. The discussion of Cao Pi's mandate could now turn toward a Confucian discussion of the *moral* worth of past emperors.

Cao Pi refused to take up the offer in just the way that it was intended. From this point on, he made a long and subtle argument that he himself contained a certain moral essence that could not be altered: he would stand pat. That was as far as he would take the offer to reason together. And for some weeks, he proclaimed lists of divinities and serious references to passages from texts that had been underutilized, poorly compiled, and poorly understood in China for more than two or three hundred years, specifically *Zhuangzi*, *Lüshi qunqiu*, and *Huainanzi*. The result was in the end a link established by Cao Pi between himself and names from antiquity that had never before been trotted out in such contexts of royal legitimation, but were rooted deep in antiquity, before the Han and before the Zhou era, during a primitive innocence in China's past, when men chose to rule in a mystical way—through sage refusal: it was rulership by effective passivity, not by effecting rules.

This line of reasoning would be opposed by yet another bloc, consisting of a famous general and hundreds who had ridden with him. They even mentioned particularly the baseness of the advice that springs from the oracle-texts and that Cao Pi had spurned the more appropriate sages and ethical arguments.

In reflecting on Sima Yi (and including the group just mentioned), we realize that they did not demonstrate outright opposition to Cao Pi's taking the throne: such an opposition would not have been tolerated by Cao Pi at this counsel. They did, however, show the rest of the political public that the matter of Cao Pi's intellectual moods and commitments in something as important as his ruling image needed to be more gracious to the community of like-minded Confucians, men who desired to protect their culture.

Cao Pi thus, on the moment of taking the throne, was branded by important families as an incautious intellect. Cao Pi forged ahead in his style, nevertheless, unwilling to yield them ground. This would have extremely important ramifications in the coming three decades, as Cao

Pi's policy decisions frequently overturned those of his father, including his father's court personnel appointments. Ritualist debates continued with even more passion under his son's reign, and the Simas, with a number of allies, succeeded in grasping the dynasty away from the Caos. It is ironic that they were enabled to do so by using pro-Cao Cao arguments at various junctures. They saw the Cao-family dynasty as offering an unwieldy mélange of Cao Pi policies and intellectual attitudes that denigrated not just the Han, not just other scholars and the political public, but also Cao Pi's own father. There was probably some kernel of truth to it, and Cao Pi's stylized gestures of father worship in 220 could not stave off the ill will that his policy and ritual reversals of Cao Cao brought on.

TWO FAMILIES WHO COPED WITH POLITICAL AND CULTURAL CHANGE

In a brief examination of two nonroyal families, we find profound differences along with points of similarity. The Wangs are an example of the political public of the old center-south, west, and northeast during the Han era. Very many of the leading families there rose as administrators in provincial locales; they suffered lack of continuity because of the lapses in central government and the sufferings under the eunuchs during the 160s and 170s; and they often sent their sons to study the Confucian classics with famous masters who commanded the loyalty of hundreds, sometimes thousands, of students. After about 180, we frequently see men of this sort declining the posts given them by the central court and garnering their local resources instead. The Yus, whom we examine following the Wangs, on the other hand, sprung from a southern culture that began to take root through the Eastern Han period. Southern families tended to be large, and the economies of the several southern centers remained fairly healthy. The foremost families' strategy was directed to maintaining their estates. They were not recipients of the same sort of career path that we find among the Wangs, and they kept their military resources consistently at the ready. Their relationships with the Sun-family military overlords, who dominated the coastal south of China from about 200, were mercurial and often dangerous. Sun Quan in particular was an erratic ruler, given to violence in his court meetings, and impatient with the more sober of his courtiers.

The Wangs of Donghai

Prior to Wang Lang himself (c. 165 to 228), we know almost nothing of the Wang family of Dan, in Donghai commandery (southwest Shandong, between Suzhou and the coast). Sometime in the 180s, Wang took leave of what was probably his first post in the Eastern Han government to mourn for his former teacher, Yang Si, a renowned classical scholar. Around this time he was nominated to *maocai* status (as was Cao Pi early in his career). He came to prominence in the 190s as Grand Administrator of Guiji commandery (present-day Ningbo area of Zhejiang), which late in Eastern Han was the most important intellectual and political locale in the southeast.

Wang Lang was typical of educated men after the 150s who applied themselves increasingly to independent learning, debates, and new writing genres; many became widely known for their reformist stances. At Loyang and in the provinces, teachers and their students (sometimes legions of them) became politically active. The more serious wrote exegeses not only on the canon of Confucian scripture, but also on works of history, and sometimes Daoist philosophy, ritual, and legend. Such leading lights as Xun Shuang and Zheng Xuan (both dead by 200 C.E.) were attempting to interpret ritual, history, and philology often with antiestablishment or other political motives in the background. Devotion to one's teacher and to broad learning and grand syntheses became marks of the reformist leaders. Such men were overtly political (even when in reclusion) and frequently placed by their contemporaries into political categories: for example, "pure officials" (*qingguan*, that is, officials usually associated with court ritual, education, and administration, and free of eunuch and empress-family links); anti-innercourt activists; and "proscribed" (martyrs who had been persecuted and exiled by the court). Wang Lang also displayed conservative Confucian traits: in his capacity as grand administrator of Guiji he dissuaded a local cult from continuing the use of engraved wooden images of Qin Shihuangdi.

In 194, facing an impending assault by Sun Ce (older brother of Sun Quan), he was advised to flee by his local mentor Yu Fan (*see below*). But Wang thought it was his duty as a Han imperial official to defend the area, and he did so, with a weak campaign along the coast. He was defeated in 196, but did not escape the notice of Cao Cao and was recommended to the Han court (now controlled by Cao Cao in Xu) for such posts as Grandee Remonstrant and Consultant in the military office of the Minister of Public Works, and Libationer in the army (around 217). From that time on he received no further military offices. In 217 he was made Privy Treasurer, but already, from about 215 (perhaps concurrently) until about 220, he was Grand Master of Ceremonies (one of the Nine Ministers), an office that supervised the training and activities of court astrologers, schools, compilations, and rites and became an important post for his son as well. When Cao Pi became king (not yet emperor), Wang Lang was made Grandee Secretary (April 220), and just before the

220 imperial rites for Cao Pi, he was made Grand Judge, another ministership. The Nine Ministers were posts traditionally at the pinnacle of civilian positions in the Eastern Han court.

Wang Lang cited the Confucian classics consistently in his court memorials, with special emphasis on the *Book of Changes* (*Yijing*). He wrote commentaries on several of the Confucian classics. And once again, as we saw in the case of the new emperor Cao Pi, by investigating the rich strata of belles lettres of China—official and private essays and letters collected and transmitted for centuries—we get a convincing snapshot of Wang Lang's intellectual passion. He wrote one of the most important texts of the year 221, namely, a commemoration spoken probably earlier during Cao Pi's legitimation counsel but ultimately carved into the dynastic announcement (mentioned earlier) that was erected near Xu.

At one point in this text, Wang Lang (and, indirectly, several others who attached their names to the speech) mildly chastised Cao Pi for the unruly Daoist-sounding omens and divinities that he used for his delay in taking final dynastic steps in the Han's abdication. During the counsel discussions, Cao Pi had also been opposed by Sima Yi and others for accepting political omens and for propagating new Zhuangzi-style heroes instead of the more trustworthy Confucian examples. Thus we read here:

> We are aware that the *Yijing* calls a sage [one who] "makes profferment to heaven's seasons" and *Lunyu* says that a "superior man stands in awe of the mandate of heaven." Heaven's mandate dismissed and appointed [in the beginning]; [but] subsequently emperors abdicated [directly] to each other. For this reason, Yao's abdicating to Shun was [because] the mandate resided in him [personally]. And Shun's acquiescing to Yao we call receiving the endpoint [of a cycle]. Yao knew that the mandate of heaven had dismissed him and thus he *had* to abdicate to Shun. [Shun] knew that epochal reckoning had come to reside in him himself, and thus he did not dare *not* to accept. Having to abdicate is "profferment [that is, offering one's self humbly] to heaven's seasons," and having to accept is "awe of the mandate."[4]

Wang Lang thus used the more traditional classics to appeal to a philosophy that says kings should take up their duty as a part of their fate—one that is determined by epochal cycles whose movements trump our powers to reason about them.

Farther along, he had this to say, in reference to Cao Pi's continued refusal of the throne: "The perished have numens (or, undying spirits). Thus Shun surely was angry in his spirit-tomb at Cangwu. Da-Xia surely was melancholy at Shanyin, in Guiji (where he died). The Martial King (that is, Cao Cao) surely was unhappy in Gaoling Murky Palace. That is why we dared make request on pain of death."[5]

This comment revisits Cao Pi's earlier signal that the soul of Cao Cao, his famed father, could be linked to the omens that portended well for Cao Pi. Here Wang Lang has placed Cao Cao, grumbling in his tomb, in the same category as the hero–founders of Chinese civilization, who also grumbled about Cao Pi's behavior. It is indeed a stretch that Cao Cao, only dead for several months, was part of a cheering squad for Cao Pi that included Yao and Shun, but it probably had rhetorical impact and it supported Cao Pi's own attempt at this, as described earlier.

Wang Lang's text mentioned scores of omens that verified Cao Pi's anointment by heaven to be emperor. But it is important to point out that these omens were not the dangerous, unanchored omens brought by Daoists from Sichuan or political oracle-texts, as Cao Pi had preferred. Instead, they reflected the way anointment by heaven was handled in the Confucian classic *Liji*: the appearance of sweet dew, *zhi* mushrooms and essence-springs, white tigers and leopards, trees with joined roots, and more.[6] Wang thus placed his old-line scholar's stamp of approval on Cao Pi's deliberations, but he also left a bit of wiggle-room for Cao Pi's oracle-texts and omens. Wang merely wanted Confucian values to assume priority.

Wang Lang had already been made Grandee Secretary in the spring of 220. His noble title was advanced when Cao Pi took the throne at the end of that year, and his income-households increased greatly after 227, when Cao Pi's son was crowned as the Emperor Ming. Finally, he was posthumously awarded a temple name and a placard in the imperial temple in August of 243—a high state honor.

We must ask two questions thus far: did Wang Lang's famous 221 inscription urging Cao Pi toward the throne, while firmly drawing a philosophic position by which Cao Pi should define himself, make him a pro–Cao Pi loyalist, or, instead, at least a figure slightly sympathetic with Sima Yi and others who were taken aback by the political culture fostered by Cao Pi? Moreover, was Wang's use of the classics mere window dressing, or was he maintaining a principle? To address these questions, we can look at some facts about Wang Lang's sons and grandsons.

Wang Su (195–256) was born in the worst moment of his father's struggle to extricate himself from military defeat along the coast. When Cao Pi was considering taking the Han throne, Wang Su was only twenty-five and had not yet risen to important posts. It is significant that Wang Su's career in the Cao-led new dynasty consisted almost purely of civilian offices, not military campaigning, although he acted well on several occasions early in his career as military adviser. Sometime just prior to 220, his father sent him to study with the famous scholar Song Zhong, and by the early 240s he had held such posts as Inspector of the Imperial Library, scholar in the Chongwen Observatory (functioning as a type of document-intake center for the court), and finally Grand Master of Ceremonial, an office his father had also held. At that point, though, Wang Su suffered a setback at the court, which was dominated by Cao Shuang, regent for a young Cao emperor: Wang Su had pursued ideas about scholarship and ritual even though he ran up against men approved by Cao Shuang, and was sent away to be Grand Administrator in the Guangping commandery. He was brought back about 245, and received appointments as Superintendent of the Imperial Household (in 249) and Grand Master of Ceremonial again, which posts he held almost until his death in 256.

Wang Su made his mark in the classics and in court ritual controversies (specifically, he was involved in a decades-long discourse about the late Zheng Xuan's classical commentaries, which he opposed). Wang Su wrote on nearly all the classics including Daoism, and essays on Confucian legends, phonetics, and lexicology. But besides his writings on the classics, one of his most effective actions concerned his fight to improve the hierarchical position of court scholarship. While head of the Imperial Library, he made a reasoned plea that it be freed from subordination to the Privy Treasury, as it had been for much of the Han, when it was dominated by eunuch scribes. Having won his policy recommendation, the library became subsumed under the Master of Ceremonial's office, and Wang Su never rose higher than Grand Master of Ceremonial, even though his family's loyalty, his connections, and reputation gave him great opportunities to do so.

As an activist for court scholarship, he made a strong mark in an office that had suffered discontinuity for years. He extended its purview to the Imperial Academy, its scholars, the library, the ritual calendar, omen interpretation, and the examinations of officials. This gave him the needed resources to further his and his family's scholarly influence. In 246, the Cao court proclaimed Wang Su's teachings on the classics as official for examination preparations and his writings were even quoted by the boy-emperor at the court Academy in 256. But Wang Su specifically proclaimed that for study of the classic *Book of Changes*, his father's commentary, which Wang Su had amplified, was to be made the official one.

Wang Su produced more sons than his father did, mostly because the years from about 220 to the 250s were relatively more peaceful and far more organized politically. Yet none of his own sons became renowned for scholarship. One of them served in the state government and studied the classics and gave memos to the throne on ritual, but there is little further information. Two of his other sons were known for military achievements, one of whom was infamous for having murdered female servants. Wang Su's daughter, however, became highly educated, was praised as such by her grandfather, Wang Lang, and went on to marry Sima Zhao, father of the founding emperor of the next dynasty.

With the marriage of a Wang daughter into the Sima family, one that had been waiting in opposition to the Caos for decades, we return to the matter of Wang Lang's political position. We may speculate, with good circumstantial evidence, that even then, in the winter of 220–21, Wang Lang knew full well that his old-fashioned classicism and appeals to a legitimizing rationale that drew on a philosophy of heavenly mandate placed him in the camp of the entrenched opposition—with such men as the Simas, the Zhongs, and the Xuns of Yingchuan, all challengers of Cao power. As further evidence, sometime around 220, he had supported politically the man whom he designated as his son's classics master, Song Zhong, because the Song's son was yet another of those executed by Cao Pi in the Wei Feng purge. The Wangs of Donghai were leaning against the Cao current all along, and their relations with the Simas' new dynasty (founded in 266) were thus secured more easily.

The role of learning and the classics, finally, we must judge as having been significant and layered in principles and values, even though changing times would keep later descendants from making their marks as scholars. Wang Lang's quotations of the *Yijing* probably were not window dressing, since his commentary on that classic was considered valuable and placed inside court educational offices. His family remained successful and well known only through scholarship, mostly the type of scholarship that is associated with the court and its ritual needs. Wang Su, we have seen, probably passed up higher honors and ranks under the Caos in order to devote himself to those court offices. Su's ritual studies were still quoted and studied even centuries later, as the founders of the Tang dynasty carefully established themselves in the seventh century as legitimate heirs to and appliers of ritually correct rule.

The Yus of Guiji

A Yu family descendant, in the decades following Yu Fan's (164–233) death, organized Yu Fan's and others' pertinent writings and circulated them privately as a kind of biography. The text of it would have been of interest to the Wu ruling family, particularly Sun Quan, who had brought Yu to court on numerous occasions and who had just proclaimed himself as emperor (r. 229–252) of Wu at the revitalized Jiankang (near modern Nanjing). The work was read by writers and historical compilers for centuries, and in the fifth century long extracts were placed into a commentary on the Three Kingdoms' standard history, as were many of the quotations above, and thus preserved to this day.

Wang Lang's official duties as Grand Administrator of Guiji had taken him directly into the Yu family area, and so it is not surprising that Wang had Yu Fan close to him as adviser: the Yus were one of the several most powerful families there. We know through facts from the Yu Fan "biography" and elsewhere that early Yus had received Han court appointments as administrators in southern commanderies and towns, even as far south as modern Vietnam, but by Yu's time, and even more so after his death, family members consistently maintained estates and offices in Guiji.

Yu Fan himself was appointed early in his career to the Guiji Bureau of Merit, and later as Headman of nearby Fuchun, and had hosted Sun Ce at their estate in Guiji. He turned down appointments that would have brought him to the Cao-led court in the north. He was widely hailed as scholar, *Yijing* diviner, medicinalist, and author of commentaries on Confucian classics as well as the *Laozi* and *Taixuan*, and essays on harmonics and astronomy. In fact he was acquainted with leading mathematicians and mathematical astronomers in the south. This marks a distinction from the type of learning seen in the Wang family (and generally among the northern elite), and there are other distinctions that I touch on below. Politically, Yu Fan was separated from the world of Wang Lang. Yu, although nominally assisting a Han-court appointee in the 190s (and thus indirectly beholden to the Cao Cao cause) was involved politically only with the Wu court. Yu Fan had no role in the counsel that Cao Pi staged in 220–21 with representatives of the leading families, even though southern families had been represented there. Yu Fan was of another world—deeply entrenched as a southern landed magnate and courtier.

At the time that he finished his work on the classic *Yijing*, Yu Fan made a long statement about his education and his scholarly commitments. In it he mentioned that his commentary was based on the text of the classic that was passed on from his great-great-grandfather's day, and that this version of the classic had an old Western Han "school" pedigree. Then Yu adds:

> I happen to have been born in a chaotic world and grew to manhood in military action. I studied the classics [i.e., specifically the *Yijing*] between the calls of the drum and rehearsed my essays aloud, riding on cavalry horseback. I avoided the explanations of the former [*Yijing*] commentators and produced my commentary based on the text of the classic itself [i.e., the version handed down in his family]. In addition, when I was a provincial official in Chentao I dreamt that I met a Daoist master. He let down his hair and it covered his deerskin coat. He laid out six lines for an *Yijing* divination and then wiped away three of them in order to set out drinks for me. I pleaded that he use the whole [six lines]. The Daoist master said

"the *dao* of the *Yijing* is in the heavens, so [even a mere] three lines are sufficient."

How is it that my fate in life has been to take up the mastery of this classic? All the different [commentative] schools and explanations that I have read are run of the mill. Their interpretations are unfounded, and they change what is established just so as to give their corrections.[7]

From this point forward, Yu Fan sets out severe criticism of the best known of Eastern Han scholars: Xun Shuang, Ma Rong, Zheng Xuan, and Song Zhong. The latter (who died around 220) was the favored classics master of Wang Lang and his family. Writing about and interpreting the classics was an activity of the political public and could lead to associations and connections and high office. Yet Yu Fan was highly self-confident as a type of "professional" scholar, pitting himself against the most respected in the field.

Yu Fan was also famous for writing about and promoting Guiji's leading contributors to Chinese culture, emphasizing their scholarship. He was, in a sense, a big local booster, and was known to have communicated his sentiments to scholars of the north, including Wang Lang. Although we can thus be assured that Guiji was not totally remote, we must also take into consideration the fact that the area was quite different in the types of learning being promoted there.

A first sort of difference has to do with the view of the *Yijing* classic as a book of hands-on mystery. Yu Fan made *Yijing* divinations, often at the Wu court, and often concerning upcoming battles and other decisions, in the most ancient of Chinese traditions that called for shamanlike fortune-tellers at ruling courts. He took this role seriously and did not shrink from speaking out harshly against the Wu court when required. For doing so, he was exiled for a full ten years to a post in Jiaozhou, far away in the south, where he was said to have had hundreds of disciples. In our anecdotal and court records surrounding the northern courts—both the failing Eastern Han emperors and the courts of their military overlords—no such figure emerges. We do learn of this sort of divination with men like Guan Lu (see Chapter 4) and earlier the Daoist representatives and readers of the mysterious oracle-texts. But those men were not from the great leading families. These families produced scholars, and some of them treated the Daoist works and the *Yijing*, but none of them did so in the context of telling fortunes at court—that was a southern phenomenon.

Moreover, Yu Fan wrote his *Yijing* commentary sometime between 195 and 210, yet afterward, probably during his years of exile, he produced works that dealt with the mathematics that underlay the classic correlations with the Chinese pitchpipe tonal system and the calendar. Guiji was a nexus of mathematical scholarship: Kan Ze of Guiji (d.

c. 250), who once sought instruction in *Yijing* divination from a well-known teacher, then rose to an official position at the Wu court and tutor to the Wu heir apparent, was a student of the most famed mathematical astronomer of the previous generation—Liu Hong of Guiji; and Lu Ji of Guiji (d. 219) was known for his intense study of astronomy and mathematics. He produced works on the *Yijing* and *Taixuan* texts, including its astronomical correlations, and a work on star maps. A particular in-law descendant of Yu Fan—strongly committed to the Yu family—wrote an important work on astronomy. Such a center of numerical and astronomical scholars also was a southern phenomenon.

CONCLUSION

Thus, it is possible, and even effective, to speak of a political public in the late-Han and post-Han periods: it was a salient feature of society and politics. A key type of lettered men and women (from various levels) had already been emerging for some time, but the group grew especially charged when the political and social order collapsed. The politically minded were called upon to form groups, to act, and to strive.

It is important to see these men and women for what they were—not too unlike us, and not essentially mysterious, sagelike, evil incarnate, or other such moralistic icons. They traveled, stayed at guest lodges, and observed curious sites. They read documents and placards, and conversed in urban centers, especially the capitals. When visiting the provinces, they would have had opportunities to enter an estate and view illustrations on shrines and tombs or read inscribed memorials. They were educated in the classics and writing, yet also knew a good deal about other things, such as calligraphy, engineering, agriculture, art production, and warfare. In addition, the different regions of China, although islands of uniqueness on a vast continent, nonetheless reached out culturally to one another. This was the same process that occurred in prehistoric China, when civilization centers (typically the kernels of the later regions) reached toward one another, only later to be cordoned off as enemy states.

We can see that choice in public and private affairs was within the horizon of this public, no matter whether high achievers from low origins, or only middle bureaucrats from high origins. In the instance of the former, Cao Pi, the push and pull of his peers and associates mattered in political moments. This top man, although a military overlord, was not able to make his rule, or its style and dispensations, sit well over large areas unless he took counsel with peers in the various locales and from different levels of support, including a once-threatening army of Daoists.

Such interplay of policy and intellect in the shaping of a dynasty may fly in the face of conventional wisdom about this period, which has so frequently been considered an era merely of military coercion and ineluctable economic forces.

With Wang Su as an examplar of the middle bureaucrat, an even more complex situation is involved. Wang could very well have striven for a higher office. But, if our deductions are correct, three things fixed his choice at the level where he could claim leadership in scholarship. One was that his family was tipping gradually toward the Simas and away from the Cao spotlight (in fact, they become fixed to the Simas in the next generation). Another was that scholarship in China in this period, and in others, was not merely an all-nighter before the SAT test that later brings the diploma. It was an outlet for writers and orators to influence one another and their rulers through history, the classics, and court ritual and policy. It reflected a family's well-practiced method for preparing their sons (and occasionally daughters) for a politically active life. Thus, Wang Su's devotion to a high but not the *highest* office gave him a platform from which he could honor his father's scholarship as well as his own. Finally, he was, simply speaking, committed to his convictions about texts and policies. To view Chinese culture and politics in this light is refreshingly nonmaterialist and points up the role of sometimes wavering, sometimes conflicting passions about ideas that ranged from purely technical contexts to political struggles.

NOTES

1. Howard L. Goodman, *Ts'ao P'i Transcendent*, 81.
2. Ibid., 105–6.
3. Ibid., 112.
4. Ibid., 198.
5. Ibid., 199.
6. Ibid.
7. Howard L. Goodman, "Exegetes and Exegeses of the Book of Changes in the Third Century A.D.: Historical and Scholastic Contexts for Wang Pi" (Ph.D. dissertation, Princeton University, 1985), 66–68.

SUGGESTED READINGS

Crespigny, Rafe de. *Northern Frontier: The Policies and Strategy of the Later Han Empire*. Canberra, 1984.

_____. *Generals of the South: The Foundation and Early History of the Three Kingdoms State of Wu*. Canberra, 1990.

Fang, Achilles. *The Chronicles of the Three Kingdoms (220-265)*. Cambridge, MA, 1965.

Goodman, Howard L. *Ts'ao P'i Transcendent: The Political Culture of Dynasty Founding in China at the End of the Han*. Seattle, 1998.

CHAPTER 4

Biography of Guan Lu

Andrew Meyer

The interaction between the realm of human affairs and the surrounding universe of seen and unseen phenomena was a constant concern for the Chinese from the earliest times. As we saw in the story of Fu Hao, cosmological thought played a significant role in politics and society from the Shang dynasty on. By the third century of the Common Era, China's social and political order had gone through significant changes, as previous chapters have shown. But the concern with a cosmic context for human affairs remained important.

In his discussion of the life of Guan Lu, Andrew Meyer, assistant professor of history at Brooklyn College, shows how powerful ideas about the cosmic order could be. In a time when China was largely dominated by great aristocratic families, it was still possible for someone of relatively minor status to rise high in the world of courtly life through a knowledge of, and skill at deploying, cosmological thought.

To understand fully the complexity of Chinese culture it is vital to have a sense of how people perceived and understood the world around them. Meyer sets out Guan Lu's cosmological ideas as part of his overall life story and explicates key terms in Chinese thought and philosophy in the process. Although these concepts may be unfamiliar at first, a careful reading of this chapter will provide a useful guide to an important dimension of premodern Chinese life.

Guan Lu (209–256 C.E.) is not a name that even well-educated Chinese men and women would recognize today, but there is much evidence to suggest that he was, at one time, very famous. Guan earned his celebrity for his skill as a diviner, an astrologer, a medium, and a scholar of the occult. He is a figure who, like Erik Jan Hanussen or Uri Geller,* poses unique challenges to a historian of culture. In reviewing the testimony of Guan's life, one can only scratch one's head and wonder how much of what is attributed to him is the result of sham, showmanship, charisma, or hyperbole. One is gripped by the eerie sense that some aura of the paranormal must have clung to him. Otherwise the degree of fame he

---

*Hanussen and Geller were famous and controversial psychics in Europe in the twentieth century.

achieved in such a staggeringly crowded field is difficult, if not impossible, to explain.

Guan was born in the closing decades of the Han dynasty (204 B.C.E.–220 C.E.) and lived as an adult during the Three Kingdoms (220–265 C.E.) period, when China was divided into three separate and perpetually feuding principalities. His age was rocked by successive social, political, and economic cataclysms. Intellectual culture was in a state of ferment, long and deeply held values were being called into question, and bold new ideas proliferated. Members of social groups that had been marginalized during more stable times could approach the highest echelons of power and exert unprecedented influence.

The chief source for Guan's life is his biography in the "Wei shu" (Book of Wei) section of the *Record of the Three Kingdoms*, the official history of the period compiled by Chen Shou (233–297). The official biography has been thoroughly supplemented by Pei Songzhi's (372–451) later commentary on the text. Pei's chief source, in turn, was the "Separate Biography of Guan Lu," a reverent account written by Guan's younger brother, Guan Chen.[1] We are thus possessed of good (albeit somewhat biased) contemporary testimony about Guan Lu's life and times.

Guan's biography appears in a chapter dedicated to the "occult arts." This was a traditional and standard bibliographical genre in the early histories, dating back to the first official history, Sima Qian's (145–86 B.C.E.) *Records of the Historian*.[2] Literate men specializing in arts such as divination, medicine, spirit mediumism, geomancy, and various forms of magic had been classed under the common rubric "*fang shi* (occult scholars)" since the Former Han (204 B.C.E.–6 C.E.). The name was applied to a very eclectic assortment of individuals who did not evince any awareness of a shared identity or common purpose. However, they were alike in generally coming to suffer the low esteem of the more elite members of Later Han (25–220 C.E.) political society. In the more fluid social environment of the Qin (221–207 B.C.E.) and Former Han, many occult scholars had risen to positions of prestige and influence. As the impact of Confucianism on Han political culture grew, however, only those scholars proficient in the Confucian classics and the more refined pursuits of poetry and literary prose could claim legitimate credentials for public service. Occult scholars continued to find employment at court, but their access to the highest centers of power was severely limited.

Given this context, the dizzying heights of fame Guan Lu achieved in his own lifetime are exceptional. We might initially be skeptical of Guan's supposed celebrity, as much of the evidence for his life comes from the near-hagiography written by one of his kin. Yet other evidence supports the testimony of Guan Chen. Even excluding the excerpted material from the "Separate Biography of Guan Lu," Guan's official biography is longer and more detailed than that of any other *fang shi* recorded in the official histories by several orders of magnitude. Guan also appears independently as a figure in other portions of the *Record of the Three Kingdoms* and the subsequent *History of the Jin*.[3]

Guan's celebrity echoed for many centuries after his death. Anecdotes about Guan are compiled in famous medieval anthologies such as the *Shishuo xinyu* and the *Shoushen ji*.[4] The figure of Guan Lu continues to appear in the official histories of later dynasties. His "Separate Biography" was still in circulation as late as the Tang dynasty and is listed among the works held in the Tang imperial library.[5] He eventually became a stock figure in the literary language of the historian. Many diviners are described in the standard histories as "unsurpassed even by Jing Fang (77–37 B.C.E.) or Guan Lu."[6]

Guan's origins are somewhat obscure. He was born in Pingyuan prefecture, in what is today Shandong province. The region had once been part of the kingdom of Qi, an area famed for producing scholars of the occult arts. Guan's early interest in these subjects thus might have been the product of a long-standing local or family tradition. His biography mentions that his father "served in Licao" and "was the head of Jiqiu in Langya."[7] Thus it would seem that Guan was not the first in his family to acquire a government post (as was often the case with *fang shi*). It is unlikely, however, that his family had been of empirewide prominence for any length of time. Guan's father (whose name is never recorded in Guan Lu's biography) was in all probability the first member of the Pingyuan Guans to serve in government, though the family may have been locally prominent for its occult scholarship for many generations previous. Guan *père* almost certainly received the call to serve as a local magistrate during the chaotic days in the wake of the Yellow Turban rebellion (184 C.E.), when the dynasty experienced critical manpower shortages and many to whom the doors of power had always been closed entered government. If the Guan family could boast a long lineage of official forbears, it is well-nigh unthinkable that Guan Chen would have failed to mention that fact in his "Separate Biography of Guan Lu." Indeed, the initial motivation for writing that text may well have been to secure the legacy of Guan's fame so that the Pingyuan Guans could continue to bask in his reflected glory and enjoy something of the elevated status procured for them by Lu's meteoric rise.

The disparity between the opening of Guan's official biography in the *Record of the Three Kingdoms* and Guan Chen's account in the "Separate Biography of Guan Lu" is strikingly revealing of the traditional status accorded to men of Guan Lu's profession. The *Sanguozhi* informs us: "Guan Lu, styled Gongming, was a native of Pingyuan. His physical appearance was coarse and ugly, and he seemed to have no sense of decorum whatsoever. He would drink heavily, eat like a glutton, and always laugh and joke. Since he paid no heed to avoiding improprieties, people developed a fondness for him but lacked respect." By contrast, the "Separate Biography of Guan Lu" states:

> When Lu was only eight or nine years old he had already demonstrated a fondness for gazing up at the sky's traveling lights. Whenever he found someone who knew the skies, he would quiz him about the stars' names, and at night Lu was seldom willing to go to sleep. His parents forbade this stargazing, but ultimately they could not stop him. Lu himself would say, "Though I am young, it is a feast for my eyes to look upon the sky's patterns." He often argued, "If creatures no nobler than barnyard chickens and wild geese can recognize times, is it not obvious that humans could?"
>
> Whenever Lu was playing on a dirt field with his neighborhood friends, he would draw maps of the celestial star fields on the ground, and add the sun, moon and planets. He was able to answer any and all questions asked of him and expound at length on astrological events.[8]

The first excerpt, from the *Record of the Three Kingdoms*, reflects the traditional contempt in which classically educated scholars held scholars of the occult. It is rare for anyone deemed worthy of entry into the official histories (excepting perhaps those notorious for some infamous act of treachery or cruelty) to be portrayed in such a negative light. This kind of denigration is reserved for Daoist priests, Buddhist monks, and other such "undesirables" whose historical importance requires that their presence in the official chronicles be tolerated. By contrast, Guan Chen's account is much more typical of an opening of an official biography. It is quite conventional for such accounts to begin with a description of the subject's precocity in childhood, an early indication of the fame that he would eventually achieve, thus meriting inclusion in the official history of the dynasty. The compilation of the *Record of the Three Kingdoms* began about thirty years after Guan Lu's untimely demise, thus Guan Chen may well have had access to the official biography of his elder brother that was to be included in the chronicle. This would further explain the need that he felt for composing a "Separate Biography." Chen hoped to secure for his brother (and by association, his family) the dignity that would normally be accorded to the subject of an official biography.

Guan Chen's impulse to defend his brother's credentials posthumously corroborates an assessment of Lu's humble beginnings and reaffirms the uniqueness of his extreme success. Though occult scholars were not, as a rule, among the power elite of Later Han China, they were by no means rare. Although it is difficult to determine with certainty, it seems likely that the majority of literate people during the Han (and earlier times) would have been classified as "occult scholars" by authors of the official histories. The classically trained literati who presided over the Han court made up a thin crust of superelite individuals deeply steeped in the officially sanctioned curriculum. Locally prominent families whose scholarly interests were much more eclectic led the wider society of the empire. At all times during the Han, droves of these *fang shi* thronged the court, searching for patronage and government employment. Though their training did not (in the eyes of Confucian officials) merit them positions of real responsibility, the services of different occult experts were often employed for divination, medical treatment, exorcism, and the design of temples, palaces, and tombs. With the increasing opportunities for advancement in the wake of the Han collapse, the normal proliferation of occult scholars in the capital was amplified. As Guan Chen describes the situation at the time of Lu's death: "Now, technicians of these [occult] systems can be divided into over one hundred different schools, and their writings are voluminous, filling many thousands of chapters. Nonetheless, the world sees the coming of very few prominent men."[9]

The mystery of Guan Lu's outstanding fame under these circumstances compels an investigator to search for some identifiable pattern, some chain of events that can explain his move from obscure local magician to empirewide celebrity. The historian Pei Songzhi, whose excellent commentary to the *Sanguozhi* provides us with our most detailed information about Guan, recognized that Lu was a figure around whom a bevy of anecdotes and outright legends were inclined to collect. Aside from including what seems to be most of the "Separate Biography of Guan Lu" in his commentary verbatim, Pei sought out another work by a contemporary of Guan's named Yan Xubo. Yan had interviewed many acquaintances of Guan Lu's, and according to Pei Songzhi, had "collected and augmented fragmentary materials from all over the land, even going so far as to take hearsay and write it into the historical record."[10] In his own desire to be thorough, Pei concluded his commentary with as many of these supplementary anecdotes about Guan that he felt discretion would allow. Pei's choices are confined to anecdotes reported by natives of Lu's home district, especially focusing upon accounts of his early career. He seems to have been guided in his selection by the same impulse that motivates the modern investigator—a desire to puzzle out a notion of "where it all began" for Guan Lu.

The first story Pei excerpts from Yan Xubo's collection proves very revealing:

> Lu first became known when he did a turtle shell crack divination for a neighborhood woman over a lost ox. He instructed her to go to the wall at its far western point, stretch her neck high, and look out for the ox among the burial mounds. Naturally, in doing so she found the ox, but then she

concluded that Lu had stolen it, and she reported him to the magistrate for investigation. Only then did people learn that Lu had gained the knowledge by means of this special art. It was after this affair that the governor of Ji Province, Pei, heard about him.[11]

There is no way of judging the veracity of this incident with any certainty, but it is strikingly suggestive on a number of counts. Even if we grant that the incident took place, whether or not Guan actually found the ox through paranormal means is only of marginal interest. Certainly, a skeptic would conclude that the old woman was right, and that Guan had first stolen the ox with the intention of producing a marvelous divination once she had enlisted his services. What rings true about the anecdote (and why, one suspects, Pei Songzhi felt it was important to include it in his commentary) is the force it possesses to explain the subsequent course of Guan's career. Something must have happened to project Guan's reputation beyond his home community. This anecdote seems to fit the bill particularly well because it concludes with Guan being brought to the attention of the authorities. The accusations of the old woman would have led to an investigation and perhaps even a court case before the local magistrate. It might have produced a buzz up and down the chain of command that eventually brought Guan Lu to the notice of Provincial Governor Pei Hui, an important early patron.

Chen Shou's narrative of Guan's life corroborates such a reconstructed sequence of events. In the text proper of the *Sanguozhi*, we read:

> At this particular time, in Lu's district people did not even have to lock their doors. Those living there did not steal from one another. The grand protector of Qinghe, Hua Biao, summoned Lu to become secretary of letters. Zhao Kongyao of Anping subsequently recommended Lu to the governor of Ji Province, one Pei Hui, saying, "Guan Lu is endowed with a magnanimous and talented nature, so he bears no enmity toward any of his contemporaries. In his ability to look upward and read the patterns of the heavens, he is the match of Lord Gan and Shi Shen. When he looks down and peruses the lines of the *Book of Changes*,[12] his meditations are equal to those of Sima Jizhu. Now, it is clear that your mind too has begun to linger in those arcane depths, your thoughts to lodge in those valleys of mystery. Lu would be well chosen for sympathetic repartee on these subjects, to assure that you reach a stage of exemplary achievement in them."[13]

Qinghe prefecture is directly adjacent to Guan's home district of Pingyuan, thus Hua Biao may in fact have been the official who sat in judgment of the case reported by Yan Xubo. Even if Guan had been tried in the Pingyuan prefectural magistracy, news of the case might very well have reached Hua Biao in nearby Qinghe. It is interesting to note that the *Sanguozhi* gives the reason for Guan's first official summons as the absence of theft in his home district. This is a standard trope in laudatory biographies of public officials, implying that even when they were not in public service, their moral example was enough to edify their whole community. Here, however, it may be a backhanded allusion to Guan's own brush with the law. In any case, there is one point on which the *Sanguozhi* and Yan Xubo agree: what finally brought Guan Lu to the attention of Governor Pei was his skill in the occult arts. Somehow (whether as a result of the court case or by other means), Zhao Kongyao, a man who evidently had the governor's ear, learned of Guan's reputation as a diviner and occult scholar. Knowing that Governor Pei also cultivated an interest in these arts, he put Guan forward as a candidate for employment.

Once again, the *Sanguozhi* and the "Separate Biography of Guan Lu" paint different portraits of Guan's career under Pei Hui. According to the *Sanguozhi*: "As a result of [Zhao Kongyao's] recommendation, Hui summoned Guan Lu to take charge of the scholarship activities in his office. When Lu was brought in to see the governor, Hui thoroughly approved of him and immediately befriended him. In fact, when the governor went on to tour Julu, he arranged to take Lu along by transferring him to the post of administrative attendant."[14]

Chen Shou admits that, at the very least, Guan had thoroughly charmed Pei Hui. However, his account implies that Pei shuffled Guan from post to post in order to have access to his company, that Guan was more of a mascot than an actual assistant. The account of the "Separate Biography" is more fulsome, describing Guan's rapid rise through the ranks of Pei Hui's staff:

> As soon as they met, Shijun [Pei Hui] and Lu rose into ethereal discourse that continued until nightfall, neither of them feeling a tinge of boredom or frustration. The weather was extremely hot at that time, so they moved their couches to the front of the courtyard beneath a tree, and they continued until the cock crowed the dawn. Only then did Lu depart. The second time Lu met with Shijun, he was transferred to the attendant post at Julu. At the third meeting, he became an attendant official at headquarters, and at the fourth he was promoted to aide-de-camp. By the tenth month, Lu had been recommended for the *xiucai* ("flourishing talent") degree.[15]

Guan Chen's description of his brother's career is more overtly salutary: leaving no doubt that Lu was moved consistently up the chain of command because of his competence and skill. On several important details, however, Guan Chen and Chen Shou agree. Both acknowledge the profound impression that Lu made upon Pei Hui (though Guan Chen sketches the scene for us in much greater detail) and both emphasize the importance of Guan's skill in the occult arts in producing this effect.

This situation of course, raises the question of why a man like Pei Hui would become so taken with a diviner, no matter how skillful. One might consider that Guan's case is comparable to that of Joan Quigley, the astrologer who enjoyed the high esteem of First Lady Nancy Reagan during the 1980–88 Reagan administration and who briefly exerted a considerable influence on White House policy. Quigley's influence, however, was based on a fortuitous contact with the First Lady. Guan Lu climbed the ranks of medieval Chinese society through a sequential series of encounters (Hua Biao, Zhao Kongyao, and Pei Hui). Time and again he was able to win the friendship, confidence, and patronage of ever-more-powerful individuals, persons possessed of the highest standards of refinement and education of their day.

The "Separate Biography" and the *Sanguozhi* correspond on another crucial detail. In 248 C.E., Pei Hui put Guan Lu forward for the *xiucai* degree, the singular honor that afforded entry into the elite ranks of Wei officialdom. Acceptance of the degree necessitated a trip to the capital, Luoyang. Guan went on to become a fixture of capital society, enjoying the same success at winning admirers there as he had in the provinces. Eventually, if we believe the accounts of both Chen Shou and Guan Chen, Lu would encounter Imperial Secretary He Yan (190–249 C.E.), for a time leader of the strongest faction in the government and hence one of the most powerful men in the empire.

It is at this juncture, with Guan's departure for the capital, that his story crosses the boundary between history and legend. We cannot hope to understand Guan Lu the person, to grasp why he was consistently so able to fascinate and overawe figures of power, influence, and prestige, unless we explore the mystique of his legend. Guan's legend accumulated even as he lived; it became a part of his social persona and preceded him into the most seminal encounters of his life. Whether or not the fantastic and phantasmagoric tales told of Guan Lu are true is, in fact, moot. To understand Guan's place in Wei society and history, we must understand what he represented to the people of his time. We must put some anecdotes about him under the glass and attempt to recover their significance to his contemporaries.

To probe Guan Lu's significance as a public figure, one must first be clear about the broader cultural basis of his status. I have consistently described Guan as an "occult scholar," because this is the closest meaningful English approximation of the term "*fang shi.*" Yet to describe Guan's concerns as "occult" invites misconception from the modern reader. In fact, a highly complex, sophisticated, and venerable body of theory underpinned Guan's work. As Guan himself is supposed to have described it, in answer to a question concerning spirit mediumism:

> When the bright sun mounts the heavens, its light circulates over a vista of ten thousand *li*. But when it enters the ground, there is not even a ray equal

to the glow of a small burning coal. The full moon of the fifteenth day illuminates the night with its clear radiance, so brightly that one can see off in the distance. But when morning comes, its shine cannot even rival that of a mirror. Now, beyond the sun and the moon, there is the systematic regularity of yin and yang. This system of yin and yang is woven into the infinite variety of things. It is in accord with this system that the birds and the beasts are undergoing endless transformations. That being so, how much more must it be true of men! By ingenuity one can gain mastery over this system and with spiritual prowess can grasp the unfathomable. The efficacy of such knowledge lies not only in matters pertaining to the living, but also in signs of the dead. It was in this manner that Du Bo rode the *qi* of fire to transport his essence, and Pengsheng employed the transformations of the water elements to make manifest his form. In this way, the living can come and go; the dead can be either invisible or manifest. This is the essential *qi* of all things, the roving soul of transformations, the interactions of man and ghost, all brought about by the system.[16]

One must be familiar with the technical vocabulary of traditional Chinese cosmology to grasp the details of Guan's argument, yet certain aspects of his rhetoric are apparent at first glance. Guan begins by citing the two most obvious observable transformations of the natural world: the cyclical evolutions of the sun and moon. He then segues seamlessly to a discussion of the appearance of ghosts in the human realm. Guan's assertion is quite simple, yet forcefully stated. The appearance of the ghosts of the dead may seem extraordinary, but it is merely a manifestation of the same natural processes evident in the comings and goings of the sun or the moon. Just as the sun can go from complete obscurity to brilliant luminosity in a matter of hours, the ordinarily invisible dead emerge into substantiality if the conditions are right.

The finer points of Guan's discourse lie in the series of nested concepts to which he alludes: *qi*, *yin-yang*, and the five phases. All of these terms signify the same phenomena in varying degrees of specificity. The most general rubric is *qi* (translated variously as "vital energy," "pneuma," and "material force"). *Qi* is the basic substance of the universe, the fundamental matter out of which all perceptible phenomena are composed. *Qi* passes through a series of distinct and discernible states, the most basic of which are yin and yang. The yin state is associated with all objects or forces that are dark, cold, still, yielding, or female; the yang state corresponds to those that are bright, hot, kinetic, assertive, or male. All objects in the tangible world belong to one state or the other, but they are not mutually exclusive. The same *qi* can become either yin or yang depending upon what point it occupies in its cycle of transformation. As it evolves, *qi* further differentiates into five phases of material existence: wood, fire, earth, metal, and water. Again, no *qi* is permanently bound to any one phase, so objects continue to transform fluidly from one phase to the next.

The five phases are the most basic tangible forms of *qi*, all perceptible objects in the phenomenal world are composed of one or more of the five phases. All the sensory properties of matter—taste, color, pitch, smell, texture—arise from the inherent properties of the five phases. The color red and the taste of bitterness, for example, are associated with the phase of fire, thus wherever these qualities can be observed (whether in the color of fresh raspberries or the taste of lemon peel), it is attributable to the presence of fire *qi*. Furthermore, the evolutions of the five phases are responsible for the distinctive qualities of different areas in space and periods in time, thus the heat of the summer and the warm climate of the south are likewise attributable to the prevalence of fire *qi*. The other seasons and directions are similarly correlated to particular phases of *qi*.

These theories to which Guan Lu alludes did not originate with him. They were, by the time Guan was practicing his craft, several centuries old. They were first articulated during the fourth or third century B.C.E. and are generally attributed to a Warring States scholar named Zou Yan (fl. c. 270 B.C.E.). The ideas of Zou Yan serve Guan's claims of divinatory power for two reasons. First, the evolutions of yin, yang, and the five phases of *qi* are not random. One form yields to another according to a regular and predictable pattern. Thus, if one can identify the constituent forms of *qi* within an object or situation and one knows the universal rules of transformation, one can predict with unswerving accuracy the next object or situation that will evolve as the cycle progresses. In this respect, prognostication is less a form of clairvoyance than of deductive reasoning.

Second, within the yin-yang, five-phases system of cosmology, all objects partaking of the same category of *qi* are sympathetically and resonantly linked. Ancient scholars observed that when two strings on separate lutes were tuned to the same pitch and one was plucked, the other would vibrate in resonance with its counterpart. Since the particular pitch of the string was attributable to the prevalence of one phase of *qi* (there were five notes in the traditional Chinese musical scale, each of which was correlated to one phase of *qi*), they concluded that all objects in the universe were similarly sympathetically linked. Stimulating any object composed of fire *qi* would produce a simultaneous resonant response in all other objects also composed of fire *qi*, no matter how far removed in space. Since all objects in the universe are exchanging these resonant influences at all times, a skilled observer can reconstruct the situation of the entire cosmos at any given moment through analysis of a very small, localized set of objects or events. Ergo, Guan Lu's claim to know the location of the old lady's ox on the basis of a series of cracks produced in a turtle shell was not based on possession of some supernatural faculty. Guan understood the patterns of resonant interaction between the different forms of *qi*, thus he could read the location of the ox from the cracks in the bone because of the resonant influences exchanged between the ox, the bone, and the cosmos at large during the moment of the cracking. These cosmological theories provide the consistent backdrop of anecdotes about Guan Lu. One story in particular demonstrates the centrality of yin-yang and five-phases ideas to Guan's continuing credibility and influence. It occurs early in Guan Chen's "Separate Biography" and concerns a banquet and debate supposedly arranged by Dan Zichun, grand protector of Langya, to which Lu was invited as the guest of honor when he was only fifteen years old. According to Guan Chen, one hundred scholars appeared at the banquet to contend with the precocious young man:

> Lu presented . . . [a] question: "Those who want to face me in debate today are the scholars seated immediately around you, correct?" Zichun replied, "I want myself to address you when the banners go up and the opening drums roll." Lu said, "I have barely read through the texts of the *Odes*, the *Analects*, and the *Changes*. My learning is superficial and I cannot recall and recite verbatim the words of the sages or elaborate on events of Qin and Han times. May I limit the conversations to the nature of the five phases—metal, wood, water, fire, and earth—and of ghosts and gods?" Zichun exclaimed, "This is the most difficult of all subjects, and you regard it as easy!"
>
> And then there rang out a chorus of great debate. They threaded their way though *yin* and *yang*, with literary embellishments wafting about like blossoms and the subjects of discussion sprouting in every direction. Rather than quote from the sages and ancient records, they concentrated on bringing to light the natural order of things. Zichun and all the assembled scholars joined the attack. The points and retorts thrust back and forth like spears. But Lu answered each and every assault with a reply that was more than adequate. They continued the entire day, until dusk fell, without even pausing for food and drink. Zichun finally addressed his guests: "This lad of only a few years overflows with a wealth of talent. Listening to his words during the debate reminded me of Sima Xiangru's rhyme-prose on traveling and hunting. How remarkable is his diversity, stamina, and spirit! One can certainly understand that these systems of heavenly pattern, earthly design, and metamorphosis are not just so much nonsensical talk." Lu was soon known throughout Xuzhou and accorded the sobriquet "Spirit Boy."[17]

That the marvelous event described by Guan Chen ever took place is highly questionable. If Lu had truly been able to prevail in such a prodigal and public intellectual duel at fifteen, it is hard to imagine that his acquiring the *xiucai* degree would have had to await his encounter at age thirty-six with Pei Hui. However, the veracity of Guan Chen's tale is again less significant than its underlying rhetorical message.

It is very plausible that Guan Lu's opponents in debate would be thoroughly conversant with five-phases and yin-yang theory. By Guan's time, yin-yang theory had long ceased to be the exclusive preserve of diviners and magicians; it had become the common currency of all literate intellectuals. Beginning in the Former Han, Confucian scholars had applied yin-yang theory comprehensively and systematically to the interpretation of the classical canon. This hermeneutic move not only produced elegant and intriguing readings of the canon, it nicely served the interests of the Han state. The assertion of a structured, orderly, and regular cosmos argued persuasively for the inevitability of a structured, orderly, and regular imperium.

One might naturally ask why, if yin-yang ideas had become so commonplace, the tale of the Langya debate would enhance Guan Lu's reputation. There would have been nothing new or compelling in Guan's mastery of these very old ideas. The answer lies, paradoxically, in Guan Lu's professed *ignorance* of the classical canon. Young Guan knew nothing of human history or culture, yet this posed no obstacle to his understanding of the underlying patterns of the cosmos. Guan stood testimony to the possibility that knowledge of the natural world and cosmic change could be *disassociated* (and applied efficaciously apart) from the artifacts of culture and history.

Herein lies the innate power and appeal of Guan Lu as a medieval cultural icon. By Guan Lu's time, faith in the classical canon and, more generally, the entire cultural legacy of antiquity had been radically undermined. The people of Guan Lu's day saw venerable political and social institutions fall into ruin; they witnessed cultural traditions that had epitomized refinement and civility savagely destroyed by a tide of brute force. A sense of absolute dislocation with the past became pervasive. Either times had changed so fundamentally as to render the inherited culture of antiquity impotent, or antiquity itself had receded so far into the past as to make its culture irrecoverable.

Guan's mastery of cosmic patterns in the absence of classical learning inspired hope in this general climate of malaise. Many leading intellectuals of the day insisted that the underlying patterns of the universe could not be accessed, as the only avenue to this end—classical culture—had proven itself degenerate and flawed. Other writers raised an even more terrifying specter: the possibility that the cosmos had no underlying pattern or structure; that the world rested on a foundation of ultimate chaos. Guan Lu was a living refutation of these disconcerting assertions. His ability to perform marvelous prognostications and acts of clairvoyance stood testimony, not only to the possibility of accessing the patterns of the cosmos, but even to the very existence of cosmic order itself.

A number of stories told of Guan Lu help us understand the consolation he might have afforded his admirers. Early in the *Sanguozhi* biography of Guan, it is recorded:

Lu's father was serving in Licao, where three brothers of a local family, that of Guo En, long suffered with a crippling foot ailment. Lu was asked to divine the source of this with milfoil stalks, and he reported, "The hexagram[18] shows your honored family's ancestral tomb, and in that tomb is a female ghost. She was your aunt, if not the wife of your father's elder brother then of his younger brother. Long ago during a period of famine someone owed her an interest payment of several cups of rice. Unable to make the payment, he got rid of her by pushing her into a well. When she screamed out, he rolled a huge rock into the well which crushed her skull. Her wandering soul craved vengeance, and she took her case personally to heaven." Upon hearing this explanation, En immediately burst into tears and confessed to the crime.[19]

On the surface, this appears to be a stock ghost story, of a kind quite commonly found in the detective fiction of more recent centuries (such as the *Celebrated Cases of Judge Dee* by Robert van Gulik). Yet in the context of Guan's time it is redolent with deeper significance. As a man who had killed a woman, Guo En was guilty of abusing his patriarchal authority. As a nephew who killed an aunt, he had contravened the natural order of family relations. Such crimes of abuse or rebellion had become all too common during the Three Kingdoms. However, through the good agency of Guan Lu and his understanding of cosmic patterns, Guo En is brought to justice.

In a fundamental sense, Guan Lu (that is, the Guan Lu of legend) has demonstrated that victims are not ultimately helpless. The murdered ghost has taken her appeal "directly to heaven." Without the intervention of a human authority, she has been able to inflict punishment on Guo En's family. Religious groups such as the Celestial Masters had popularized the promise of such divine justice during Guan Lu's lifetime. Yet Guan Lu is able to demonstrate that such justice does not depend on any institutional church or special relationship with divine powers. Retribution like that experienced by Guo En is a function of the natural patterns of the cosmos, and as such it is discernible to any layperson (like Guan) who understands those patterns and their operation.

Another legend about Guan Lu conveys a similar message:

Lu went to see the grand protector of Anping, Wang Ji, who asked him to perform a hexagram divination. Lu reported, "[A] giant serpent will appear on your bed with a brush in its mouth. Young and old alike will rush out to see it, and that will quickly drive it away. And a blackbird will fly into one of the rooms and have a raucous fight with a swallow. The swallow will die and the blackbird will leave. You can expect these . . . anomalies." Surprised by these predictions, Ji asked whether they were signs of good or ill fortune. Lu replied, "These will occur simply because this official residence is very old, and various elves and goblins from the area are playing tricks. . . . The giant serpent with the brush in its mouth is nothing more than an old recording clerk. The quarreling between the blackbird and the swallow is nothing more than the antics of an old carriage attendant. Though I can easily see the emblems of these anomalies in the hexagrams, I see no signs of impending unfavorable times. I am confident that these are not indications of contrary times." Indeed, there was no cause for concern.

And yet another legend from the "Separate Biography" of Guan Lu:

A fellow villager of Li's, Nai Taiyuan, asked him, "Some time ago you lectured on anomalies for His Honor Wang, telling him that an old recording clerk was a serpent and an old carriage attendant was a blackbird. Now in both cases they were originally men. How could they change into creatures so base? Is this something you truly saw represented in the line of the hexagram you cast or something that came from within your own head?"

Lu responded, "Had it not been from consideration of the inborn nature of these two and the Way of heaven, could I have made this explanation? Would I have dared to ignore the emblems in the lines of the hexagram, and depend on my own intuition and reasoning? The fact is, in the transformations that affect all things, constant forms do not exist, and in the vicissitudes that affect men, there is no constancy of bodily shape. Sometimes larger things become smaller, and sometimes smaller things become larger. There is certainly no question of superiority or baseness. The transformations of all things uniformly, one and all, belong to the Way. For this reason Kun, the father of the Xia dynasty founder Yu, was later transformed into a brown bear, and the king of Zhao, Ruyi, son of the Grand Progenitor of the Han Dynasty, became a blue hound. In both cases they were men of the most respectable position, and in both cases they turned into black-mouthed beasts. How much more probable in this case, when one considers that the serpent presses upon the north quarter, and the blackbird perches upon the essence of the mature *yang*, the sun. This is a sign of brightness emerging from the vanishing dark, the flowing progress of the day's white light. Is it too much to believe that a recording clerk and a carriage attendant, given their low station, transformed into a snake and a blackbird?"[20]

Again, this tale reads as a conventional "*zhi guai*," or "record of anomalies," a popular genre of the ghost story. Woven into its fabric, however, is a rather subtle rhetorical assertion. The transformations revealed by Guan Lu's divination seem initially, to Nai Taiyuan (who stands proxy for the reader), to rebel against reason. That a human being, however lowly, should change into a blackbird or snake offends conventional sensibilities. Yet Guan Lu demonstrates that these transformations make lucid sense to one who understands the deep, structural patterns of the cosmos. The blackbird and the snake are each, through the fundamental categories of yin, yang, and the five phases, resonantly linked with forces that far transcend their immediate form (the sun and the northern boundary of the universe). Thus, the clerk and carriage attendant's assumption of these shapes cannot in any way be judged a denigration of their status—quite the contrary.

At the heart of this story is a powerful message about change and its nature. The people of Guan Lu's time were experiencing profound changes that might, at times, have seemed to defy all logic and reason. They witnessed inversions so radical as to create the impression of a "world turned upside-down." Yet Guan Lu, through his divination, is able to show that all change, no matter how shocking on the surface, can be understood by reference to the deeper underlying structures of the cosmos: "The transformations of all things uniformly, one and all, belong to the Way." To the uninitiated, many changes might be taken as signs of utter chaos, but to a person of true insight (such as Guan Lu), the world can always be seen to unfold as it should and, ultimately, as it must.

Among the crowning adornments of Guan's legend is the tale of his encounter with Imperial Secretary He Yan, who was, at the time, the most powerful figure in the Wei government and an outstanding intellectual leader in his own right. Yan and his protégé, Wang Bi (226–249 C.E.), had popularized a radical new exegesis of the *Book of Changes* that overturned traditional cosmological ideas.

Han scholars had traditionally drawn elaborate correlations between the hexagrams of the *Book of Changes* and basic images in the natural world. Thus the *Qian* hexagram, composed of six unbroken lines representing pure yang, had conventionally been associated with the images of the dragon, the horse, and Heaven (to name only a few). Han scholars had read the *Changes* as denoting an objectively real relationship between the tangible form of the hexagram and the forces of the outside world. Thus, the shape of the *Qian* hexagram was taken to encode properties that were shared in common by dragons, horses, Heaven, and any other phenomena to which *Qian* was correlated.

Wang Bi, by contrast, insisted that the relations drawn by the *Changes* were purely symbolic and discursive in nature: "Images are meant to express ideas. . . . If the concept involved really has to do with dynamism, why must it only be presented in terms of the horse?"[21] The image of the horse had been borrowed by the authors of the *Changes* to convey the idea of dynamism. Never did they intend to assert an objective relationship between the horse as a thing and the form of the hexagram itself.

He Yan and Wang Bi's new interpretation of the *Book of Changes* entailed a rejection of much of yin-yang and the five-phases theory. They created a new philosophical synthesis for an age in which many had lost faith in the optimistic theories of former times. Their universe exhibited none of the deeply embedded concrete structures of the traditional Han cosmos. It was a much more fluid and amorphous place that had to be grasped subjectively and intuitively.

Obviously, He Yan's new philosophy was the antithesis of Guan Lu's more venerable perspective. In this sense, the encounter between the two men has all the dimensions of myth. It is a clash between archetypes, the collision of one worldview with another:

On the twenty-eighth day of the twelfth month, the secretary of the board of personnel, He Yan, invited Lu to visit while Deng Yang [d. 249] was in attendance. Yan said to Lu, "I have heard that your rendering of the hexagrams [of the *Book of Changes*] is subtle beyond what ordinary mortals can do, and I would like you to try a divination for me to determine if I will reach the three ducal posts of the land." He also asked, "Night after night, I dream of green flies, a dozen of them, which come and land on my nose. I try to shoo them away, but they will not leave. What is the meaning of this?"

Lu replied, "Today, your eminent position carries weight equal to the Five Sacred Peaks, and the power you wield rivals that of thunder and lightning. Still, those who embrace you for your virtues are rare indeed, whereas those who fear your awesome power are legion. Relationships of this latter sort, I am afraid, are neither cautious, respectful, nor felicitous.

[The nose is the trigram *Gen* ("Mountain"), it is "the mountain in the center of Heaven." By being high but not steep, it preserves its noble place.] The green flies you describe are rank and offensive, and they are gathering about your nose. Those who stand at dangerous heights must be overturned, and those who commit impulsive acts of valor will perish. One must contemplate the cycles of waning and waxing, the periods of rise and decline. This is why a mountain under the earth is called "Modesty" and thunder over heaven is called "Power of the Great." The import of "Modesty" is decreasing the numerous to increase the scarce. The import of "Power of the Great" is treading no path that is not a correct path. Self-sacrifice always leads to highly visible greatness, and acting wrongly always brings harm and defeat. Your Honor, I would hope that you begin by pursuing the significance of King Wen's texts for the hexagrams, line by line, and continue by contemplating the means of the interpretations and the [images] provided by Confucius. Were you to do so, your questions about ascending to the three ducal offices could be resolved, and the green flies would be driven off as well.

Deng interjected, "This is typical of the chatter of an old pedant!" To this Lu replied, "This 'old pedant' observes that your life is near its end. This 'typical chatterer' can foresee your imminent silence." Finally He Yan said, "After the passing of the new year, we should meet again."

When Lu returned to his home in Pingyuan, he repeated this entire conversation to his uncle. His uncle upbraided him for speaking too directly. Lu answered, "What is there to fear in speaking to a dead man?" Lu's uncle grew angry and said that he was demented. On the first morning of the new year, a great storm arose in the northwest, blowing up clouds of dust that darkened the skies. A little over ten days later, word reached them that He Yan and Deng Yang had both been executed.[22]

The narrative of Guan's conversation with He Yan is heavily laden with irony, for although Guan has foretold his death, He Yan himself is insensible to the deeper import of Guan's words. Yan requests a hexagram reading from the *Book of Changes*, but (unbeknownst to him) he has already provided his own hexagram reading in his dream of the green flies buzzing about his nose. Each hexagram in the *Book of Changes* is composed of two trigrams, one stacked above the other. Each trigram was traditionally taken to represent one of the basic forces or structures of the cosmos. He Yan's dream has generated two hexagrams. Because of its shape, the nose corresponds to the trigram *Gen* or "Mountain," because of its position on the face, it corresponds to the trigram *Qian* or "Heaven." Because of their provenance, Guan correlates the green flies to the trigram *Kun* or "Earth"; because of their buzzing they represent the trigram *Lei*, or "Thunder." Taken together, He Yan's dream produces two hexagrams: "Mountain" under "Earth" yields "Modesty (*Qian*, Hexagram 15)"; "Heaven" under "Thunder" yields "Great Strength (*Dazhuang*, Hexagram 34)." The two hexagrams, in turn, constitute a dual warning: "[Decrease] the numerous to increase the scarce," "[tread] no path that is not a correct path." He Yan's dream is an augury that he has accumulated too much power, and that one false move will spell his downfall.

The deeper import of the narrative lies in the diametrical opposition between Guan's hexagram reading and He Yan's new-fangled interpretation of the *Book of Changes*. Guan's exegesis is based solely on the visual form of the hexagrams, he focuses on the objective images to which the constituent trigrams of each figure have been correlated. He Yan takes the *Book of Changes* to be a symbolic, discursive system that is ultimately a product of the human mind. Guan Lu understands that the *Book of Changes* is not properly viewed as a product of human culture at all, but the revealed blueprint of the fundamental fabric of the cosmos. The trigrams and hexagrams encode real cosmic forces that underlie the deep structural affinity between He Yan's position of authority, a mountain, and the nose on He Yan's face. As Guan Lu is reported to have declared in his "Separate Biography": "Wang Bi's mystic interpretation [of the *Book of Changes*], to which He Yan subscribes, is not worth the trouble to consider. In contrast, the yin and yang interpreters have understood its very essence for a long time."[23]

Deng Yang immediately recognizes the conflict between Guan's more traditional perspective and that of his patron He Yan, and maligns Guan as an "old pedant." Thus provoked, Guan Lu, who up to this point has attempted to be tactful, blurts out that he has just forecast He Yan's doom (and by association, that of Deng Yang). He Yan seems to be oblivious to this revelation, for he declares that he will meet with Guan again after the passing of the new year (the very time when Guan eventually receives news of his hosts' execution). When berated by his uncle for speaking so bluntly with such a powerful man, Guan replies that there is no danger in offending a dead man. Guan's certainty about He's impending destruction is more that a function of his divinatory insight, although in the "Separate Biography" we are told that Guan could read He Yan and Deng Yang's fate in their physiognomy).[24] Guan knows He Yan will not heed the warning in his dream, indeed he can not even understand it, because he is so fundamentally deluded about the meaning of the *Book of Changes* and the nature of reality itself.

Guan's last great prognostication (according to his official biography) was that of his own death, at the early age of forty-six: "My forehead lacks the 'bone of life,' and my eyes lack the 'essence of preservation.' My nose is without a 'bridge of support,' and my feet lack 'heaven foundations.' My back lacks the three *jia* shapes, and the three *ren* shapes are missing from my abdomen. All these are proofs of a short life."[25] Guan's allotment was etched into his physique as surely as the location of the old woman's ox had been inscribed in the cracks in the turtle shell. His death, as had his life, stood as unswerving testimony to the tangibility and regularity of the cosmic order.

Guan Lu was, in the most pristine sense, a man for his age. Had he been born a century earlier, it is unlikely that he would even have become known outside of Pingyuan, much less been immortalized in the official dynastic histories. Yet in the political and cultural turbulence of the Three Kingdoms, Guan embodied a hope that was both old and new. Old, because he propounded theories by then quite ancient. New, in that he insisted that the organic patterns of the cosmos could be completely divorced from human culture and the vagaries of human history. Guan captured the imagination of those he encountered. His persona resonated with their yearning to rediscover a foundational order amid the chaos of cultural collapse. He was a tonic, both against the hidebound conservatives who clung to the precedents of antiquity, and rash innovators (such as He Yan) who concocted radical ideas corrosive of confidence and optimism. Guan's story epitomizes the meeting of the person with the era, and in the face of such serendipity the boundary between history and legend dissolves.

NOTES

[handwritten: questiondbl]

1. Kenneth J. DeWoskin, *Doctors, Diviners, and Magicians of Ancient China: Biographies of Fang-shih* (New York, 1983), 91–134. The original text of Guan's biography can be found in Chen Shou, *Sanguozhi* (Beijing: Zhonghua shuju, 1962), 811–29. I have relied on DeWoskin's translation of the *Sanguozhi* material except where otherwise noted.

2. Sima Qian included a chapter on "Biographies of Diviners" within his first great historical work, *Shi ji* (Beijing: Zhonghua shuju, 1959), 3215–23.

3. See, for example, Pei Songzhi's commentary in *Sanguozhi*, 673. Guan is also mentioned in the "Monograph on the Five Phases" and the "Biography of Liu Shi" in the *History of the Jin*. See Fang Xuanling, *Jin shu* (Beijing: Zhonghua shuju, 1974), 885, 1198.

4. Richard Mather, trans., *Shih-shuo Hsin-yü: A New Account of the Tales of the World* (Minneapolis, 1975), 361. Gan Bao, *Soushen ji* (Taipei: Liren shuju, 1982), 33–35.

5. Song Qi, *Xin Tangshu* (Beijing: Zhonghua shuju, 1975), 1482.

6. See, for example, Xue Juzheng (912–981), *Jiu Wudaishi* (Beijing: Zhonghua shuju, 1976), 46. Jing Fang was another famous diviner and interpreter of the *Book of Change* in Chinese history.

7. DeWoskin, *Doctors, Diviners, and Magicians*, 93, 94.

8. Ibid., 91.

9. Ibid., 128.

10. Ibid., 131.

11. Ibid., 131–32.

12. The *Book of Change*, often known to English readers as the *Yi jing* or *I Ching*, is the most influential Chinese manual of divination and cosmology. Revered as a classic by Confucians, it was also among the stock texts of occult scholars. Guan Lu was an acknowledged expert on the *Book of Change*, and is reported to have produced writings on it, which are now lost (DeWoskin, *Doctors, Diviners, and Magicians*, 128).

13. Ibid., 107.

14. Ibid., 107–8.

15. Ibid., 110.

16. Ibid., 116–17.

17. Ibid., 94.

18. Guan has consulted the *Book of Change*, using the milfoil stalks to generate a hexagram from that text. Hexagrams are six-line graphic images thought to provide guidance and insight in dealing with the mysteries of life.

19. DeWoskin, *Doctors, Diviners, and Magicians*, 94–95.

20. Ibid., 97, 99.

21. Richard John Lynn, trans., *The Classic of Changes: A New Translation of the I-Ching as Interpreted by Wang Bi* (New York, 1994), 32.

22. DeWoskin, *Doctors, Diviners, and Magicians*, 111–12. I have departed from DeWoskin's translation in the bracketed section.

23. Ibid., 111.

24. Ibid., 113–14.

25. Ibid., 126.

SUGGESTED READINGS

Dien, Albert E., ed. *State and Society in Early Medieval China*. Stanford, 1990.

Henderson, John B. *The Development and Decline of Chinese Cosmology*. New York, 1984.

Lynn, Richard J. *The Classic of Changes: A New Translation of the I-Ching as Interpreted by Wang Bi*. New York, 1994.

Mather, Richard B. *Shih-shuo Hsin-yu: A New Account of the Tales of the World*. Ann Arbor, 1976.
Nylan, Michael. *The Canon of Supreme Mystery by Yang Hsiung*. Albany, 1993.

CHAPTER 5

Quan Deyu and the Spread of Elite Culture in Tang China

Anthony Deblasi

As Anthony Deblasi, assistant professor of East Asian studies at the State University of New York at Albany and author of "To Transform the World": The Defense of Literary Culture in Mid-Tang China, notes at the outset of his chapter, the glory of the Tang dynasty is well established in Chinese history. After China had been divided for several centuries, beginning with the Three Kingdoms period around 220 C.E., a reunified empire was finally assembled by the short-lived Sui dynasty in the 580s. In 617 the Tang was founded, and it lasted nearly three hundred years before collapsing at the beginning of the tenth century. The Tang was a great age of economic prosperity and territorial expansion for China, and for much of its duration the Tang drew traders and visitors from all across Eurasia and even from north Africa.

It was an age of aristocratic power, with the imperial government being staffed by men from great families with officially sanctioned genealogical pedigrees. And yet it was also a time of social change and development. The life of Quan Deyu (759–818) both highlights the general nature of the Tang social and political order and throws special light on the rise of a new stratum of families who challenged the existing dominance of older aristocratic clans. No single individual can serve to characterize an entire era, but Quan Deyu's story provides insight into some of the most critical areas of tension and transformation in this great age of Chinese history.

The glory of China's Tang dynasty (617–907) is by now a cliché. Yet, as with most clichés, there is an important element of truth in it. When compared to the nearly four centuries of political fragmentation and military unrest that preceded it, the ruling Li family and its loyal officials created a remarkable period of stability and prosperity, at least for the elite. There are a number of ways to gauge the dynasty's success. The ability of the court to gain control of official appointments and assert its authority over the provinces beyond the capital is certainly one indicator. The extension of authority over the provinces enabled the Tang court to collect enough taxes to afford generous cultural patronage and physical expansion. The result was an empire that stretched from the East China Sea to the Pamir Mountains in Central Asia, and from Manchuria in the north to Hanoi in northern Vietnam. Religious patronage, dynastic prosperity, and expanded contact with other cultures lent the Tang a cosmopolitan air that resulted in an unprecedented flourishing of culture. Although the dynasty witnessed important developments in all the arts, it has been especially lauded as the "golden age" of Chinese poetry.

There is another important gauge of the success of a governmental system, be it a monarchy or a republic; that is, the degree to which a government can accommodate powerful interests and inspire those interests to defend it. By this measure also, the Tang imperial system succeeded quite well. A biographical study provides a useful window on how the Tang was able to accomplish this. An examination of the life of one of the most prominent scholar–officials in the late eighth and early ninth centuries can illustrate how, by the midpoint of the Tang dynasty, when the dynasty fell on hard times, men from relatively new families had achieved the height of power and became some of the dynasty's most ardent defenders. Quan Deyu (759–818) was such a man. He climbed the ladder of power to its highest point and thus became the most successful member of a newly prominent family. His life, then, allows us to glimpse two important phenomena: the Tang creation of a broader elite and the way one member of that elite responded to political crisis.

Before turning to Quan's life, however, some discussion of medieval Chinese social structure is necessary. During its first two centuries, the structure of Tang society retained the aristocratic cast of the pre-Tang period. A relatively small number of elite families dominated society. Beneath them, the vast majority of the Tang population, as with the Chinese population today, consisted of peasant farmers, but there were also the merchants and artisans necessary for the commercial activity that augmented the agrarian economy. Although there were great economic differences within these three groups, they all were certainly subordinate to the elite families that dominated society.

This elite was actually composed of two distinct groups. The most powerful element in Tang society was a group of prestigious families known as the Great Clans. These families, some of whom could trace their family trees back to the first century of the Common Era, had dominated society and government for centuries. Although some have argued that their power rested ultimately on their control of the land, they justified their position by arguing that their mastery of literary and classical learning made them morally superior to other segments of society. The longevity of these clans before the Tang was in marked contrast to the ephemeral nature of the various imperial governments during the so-called Period of Disunion.

There was, however, a lesser group of families that we must also include in the elite, because Tang officials themselves recognized them as part of it. On several occasions, the Tang government compiled registries of the country's most notable families. Lists that derive from the official compilations and arrange these families according to provincial boundaries still survive. The Great Clans with historical ties to each locality were certainly included, but lesser families that we can identify as a provincial elite (to distinguish them from the national elite represented by the Great Clans) also appear. During the course of the Tang dynasty, these locally prominent families were able to participate in national life to a much greater extent than in earlier centuries. Nevertheless, their records of service were much different from those of the Great Clans.

In addition to the Great Clans' relatively full genealogical records, historical sources indicate that large numbers of these clans' members served in high political office. For example, the second official history of the Tang dynasty, which was compiled a century and a half after its final collapse, contains genealogical tables of the Tang Grand Counselors (somewhat akin to prime ministers, though there were usually two or three of them). If we take two of the acknowledged Great Clans, we can see the quality of their service records. The tables on the Wang clan of Langye (in modern Shandong) list more than 150 men who served in the Tang government, including several Grand Counselors. Similarly, the Liu clan of Hedong (in modern Shanxi) boasted more than 140 Tang officials, including three Grand Counselors. The records concerning the provincial elites provide a much different picture. The family of Quan Deyu is a good example. The Quan family appears on the lists of prominent families that survive, but the genealogical tables suggest its level of prominence. There we find just 19 Tang officials, and Quan Deyu the only Grand Counselor that the family produced.

Quan Deyu's personal success, however, resulted largely from his ability to meet the expectations of elite society. How was this possible? The answer lies in the particular dynamics of early Tang politics. The Tang central government was, in many ways, an instrument of co-optation. In other words, it sought to secure the support and loyalty of the elite in order to stabilize its rule. The Tang emperors therefore made great efforts to make government service attractive to the Great Clans, and the result was genuine enthusiasm among them. Yet the interests of the throne and the interests of the clans were ultimately different. Emperors wished to have social status determined by service to the dynasty, but the Great Clans, as families with prestige and service records that stretched back centuries before the Tang, preferred to allow custom and social expectations to confer status. The best example of this occurred during the reign of the second emperor, Tang Taizong (r. 626–649). When the ranking of the nation's families was submitted to the throne, Taizong was appalled that it ranked historically prominent families above those who held important positions in the Tang government. Although the tension between the Great Clans and lesser elements of the elite would persist throughout the Tang years, Tang institutions and policies did succeed in providing the lesser elite access to official positions and political power. Still, provincial elites had to justify this access by acquiring the skills and education expected of government officials. In other words, they had to master the culture of the Great Clans.

Quan Deyu's life provides an example of how provincial elites were able to acquire this culture and, on occasion, scale the heights of Tang power. There are other benefits from following the course of Quan's career. Although he is not a familiar figure to most students of Chinese history, in his own day, he was at the center of Tang political and intellectual life. His career also reveals some of the challenges that successful ministers had to confront as they endeavored to govern such a complex empire. It is also true, as we shall see, that Quan emerged on the political and intellectual stage at one of the most trying moments in Tang history. His steadfast defense of the Tang and its values indicates how thoroughly these provincial elites had also been co-opted by the Tang imperium.

QUAN DEYU'S FAMILY BACKGROUND

The introduction has already provided some indication of the status of Quan's family. As one of the locally prominent families with aspirations to national prominence, it sought to conform as much as possible to contemporary social expections. Our sources indicate that the Quans also felt the need for a prestigious pedigree. Various funerary texts for members of Quan Deyu's family trace the family's history back to one of the earliest ages in Chinese history. According to these sources, Quan's most ancient ancestor was the Shang King Wu Ding (c. 1200 B.C.E.), but this is certainly not verifiable. The sources do identify several high-ranking ancestors prior to the Tang, but it is not until the early seventh century that we have a continuous genealogical line. It is worth noting that the Langye Wangs and the Hedong Lius, the Great Clans discussed above, could trace unbroken lines back at least to the third century C.E.

The Quan family's geographical center is also of some interest. The Quans were apparently associated with the region of Tianshui (in modern Gansu province). This region was on the northwest frontier of the Chinese heartland. It was therefore somewhat removed from the traditional concentrations of Great Clans. Nevertheless, the family prospered enough so that, by the Tang period, it was able to rise to some prominence. In the six generations before Quan, members of the family had held a number of important positions. Sustained success began with Quan

Rong, a sixth-generation ancestor of Quan Deyu. Quan Rong served the short-lived Sui dynasty (581–617) as Director of Pasturages. Quan Rong's son, Quan Wendan, initiated the family's Tang service, eventually serving as a prefect, a fourth-rank (out of nine) regional administrative post. The next generation saw two members of the family secure positions as vice directors in government ministries (fifth-rank posts). Quan's closer ancestors had more modest success. His fourth-generation ancestor Quan Chongben served as a district magistrate, a regional administrator a level below a prefect. Quan's great-grandfather served as a district defender, a low-ranking post with responsibilities for policing a district.

Quan Deyu owed much of his own success, however, to his father's career. Quan Gao, Quan Deyu's father, established an excellent reputation in a very trying time. He entered government service via one of the most prestigious routes. In his youth, he passed the famed "Presented Scholar" (*jinshi*) examination. Although only a small percentage of the Tang bureaucracy was recruited from this examination, those who passed it were marked as members of a privileged elite and were usually appointed to the most important positions in the bureaucracy. As a result of Quan Gao's distinction for having passed the *jinshi*, the powerful frontier general An Lushan (703–757) petitioned the court to appoint Gao as a district defender in his command. This made good sense, because the talented young official could eventually be very useful in managing An's communication with the imperial court.

An Lushan is best remembered for the massive rebellion he launched in December of 755, which nearly succeeded in overthrowing the Tang dynasty. Quan Gao's later reputation rested on the fact that he recognized An's intentions and managed to avoid becoming entangled in the rebellion through a daring ruse. To get himself and his family out of An's control, he conspired with his brother-in-law to fake his own death. After his brother-in-law went into mourning and prepared the "corpse" for burial, An Lushan released Quan's mother. The family then made its way to the south. Soon thereafter An did rebel. Although Gao never returned to active service, his integrity during this and subsequent events earned him the respect and admiration of many loyal intellectuals who had fled to the south to avoid the chaos in north China. Among his admirers were several prominent reformers, such as Li Hua (c. 715–c. 774), who would influence his son.

STAGE ONE: QUAN DEYU'S EARLY CAREER, 773–790

The sources allow us to identify several reasons that Quan Gao never returned to active service. First, his mother's ill health distracted him.

Her death soon after their flight to the south, for example, forced him into mourning. Moreover, the rebellion raging in north China cut communications between north and south for long periods of time. When news of his appointments finally got through, Quan Gao had to decline them due to his own poor health. In the midst of these troubles, however, his son, Quan Deyu, was born in 759.

Despite the chaos in the north, the south remained relatively peaceful, and therefore Quan Deyu grew up in a fairly safe environment. The first test of his character came, however, in 768, when his father died at home at the early age of forty-six. Quan Deyu's exemplary filial behavior at his father's funeral impressed his older contemporaries. Thereafter, he continued to establish himself by virtue of his learning. The biographies of most premodern Chinese intellectuals portray them as prodigies and Quan Deyu was no exception. His official biography in the *Old Tang History* (*Jiu Tang shu*), for example, indicates that he was able to compose poetry by the age of four. Although we may doubt the quality and profundity of such childhood compositions, it is clear that Quan was quite productive quite early. The same source indicates that he had written enough (several hundred pieces, in fact) to compile a literary collection, *The Collection of Youthful Ignorance* (*Tongmeng ji*), by the time he was fifteen. Although it is now lost, this youthful collection survived into the eleventh century.

The combination of his father's contacts, his own filial behavior, and his literary efforts increased his fame and made him a likely candidate for government service. Quan Deyu entered the civil service by a route different from his father's. Whereas the elder Quan had passed the *jinshi* examination, Quan Deyu used the "protection privilege" (*yin*). Under the Tang system, there were two chief ways to qualify for office. The more prestigious was via the examinations. The more common method was to rely on the patronage of a close relative who had risen high up in the bureaucracy. Since Quan's father had been appointed to a fifth-rank post, Quan Deyu was able to claim the protection of his father posthumously. Since only about 10 to 15 percent of regular civil officials achieved their positions via the examinations, this did not reflect negatively on Quan's qualifications in the least. What it does indicate, however, is that Quan's family had succeeded in becoming part of the national elite. It was now a family with a history in the examinations and one that could make use of the "protection privilege."

Quan Deyu began his career as most young bureaucrats did. He served in a series of low-ranking positions that allowed him to become familiar with official routine. He received his first position in 780 on the staff of one of his father's admirers, Han Hui (732–794), who was the Personnel Evaluation Commissioner in Henan (around modern

Luoyang). Although Quan would spend the next eight years in such posts, his reputation continued to grow.

This early period was important in his personal life as well. Quan married very well, into the prestigious Cui clan of Boling (in modern Hebei), one of the most eminent of the Great Clans. Not only was this important socially, but the connection undoubtedly brought political advantages. His father-in-law, Cui Zao (737–787), became a Grand Counselor in 786. This was not the first time that the Quans had forged marriage ties with the Great Clans. Quan's mother was a member of the Li clan of Longxi (in modern Gansu). Although socially not so prestigious as the Boling Cuis, it was the clan of the ruling family. Thus, Quan enjoyed the social connections necessary for a successful career in the mid-Tang bureaucracy.

There were also personal losses, however, during these years. Two deaths occurred that marked the end of this first stage of Quan's career. First, his father-in-law died in 787. More important, his mother passed away in the sixth month of 788. This loss had the greater impact as it necessitated Quan's withdrawal from government service, for traditionally Tang officials generally retired and went into mourning for three years when a parent died. Quan's father had already died before Quan began his career, but his mother's death thus put his official career on hold.

STAGE TWO: QUAN DEYU'S MATURITY, 791–812

By the time Quan emerged from mourning, his talent had become clear. His official biography indicates that two of the most prominent statesmen of the age both petitioned to have him appointed to their staffs. Quan, however, had already caught the attention of the Emperor Dezong (r. 779–805). He was therefore summoned to the capital in 791 and appointed first as an Erudite in the Court of Imperial Sacrifices. The next year he was transferred to the post of Rectifier of Omissions in the central government Chancellery. Although only a rank-seven post, the appointment nevertheless gave Quan a fairly high profile since Rectifiers had the responsibility of offering criticism to the throne.

It would be another quarter-century before Quan would return to the provinces. For the next twenty-five years, he would hold prestigious and sensitive posts, not just in the capital, but in close proximity to the imperial court. One of the remarkable characteristics of Quan Deyu's official career is the methodical manner in which he rose through the ranks. During his time in capital service, he suffered no serious setbacks and was promoted to the highest reaches of the bureaucracy as quickly as regulations allowed.

Quan's success is clear from the fact that he achieved the three most coveted mileposts in the Tang bureaucratic world. To understand his accomplishment, we need to become a bit more familiar with the layers of the Tang bureaucracy. The total number of government employees probably exceeded 300,000, but, at the top of this group were the regular civil officials who were responsible for making and carrying out government policy. By the middle of the eighth century, these regular officials numbered approximately 19,000. Although securing one of these posts was such a great accomplishment that not even membership in a Great Clan could guarantee it, there were clear status differences within this group. The regular officials were divided broadly into nine ranks, with rank one being the highest and nine the lowest. Most of the 19,000 regular officials held ranks between six and nine. Making the fifth rank brought significant privileges (most significantly the right to use the "protection privilege" for relatives). Only about 2,000 of the 19,000 officials held ranks four or five. The bureaucracy's stars, however, consisted of officials holding rank three and above. There were only about 200 such officials in the Tang government.

After he had finished mourning and entered capital service, Quan Deyu began his methodical rise through the ranks. While he served as Erudite and then Rectifier of Omissions, Quan held rank seven. In 794, he was promoted to the sixth rank when he was appointed Imperial Diarist. He remained at the sixth rank despite a change in title until 797. In that year, he passed the first major milestone by achieving the fifth rank as Director of the Bureau of Merit Titles. Two years later he received a minor promotion within the fifth rank. In 802, Quan was appointed Vice Minister of Rites, a very prestigious post of the fourth rank. During the subsequent five years, Quan served as vice minister in three different ministries: Rites, Revenue, and War. All of these positions were at the fourth rank. Although he flirted briefly with the coveted third rank in 807 before being suddenly transferred back to his post as Vice Minister of War, he finally made his breakthrough in 809, when he became Minister in the Court of Imperial Sacrifices. Yet, this did not mark the end of his rise. The next year, in 810, Quan was appointed Minister of Rites and concurrently a Grand Counselor. This meant that he now had direct policy-making responsibility and was a key adviser to the emperor. We can put the significance of this appointment in clearer perspective: during the 289-year history of the Tang dynasty, only 369 men became Grand Counselors.

There is another measure of the quality of Quan Deyu's career besides simply his bureaucratic rank. Tang regulations made a distinction between two types of offices. The most prestigious ones were those described as "pure" (*qing*). These were contrasted with "tainted" (*zhuo*) offices. Tang officials believed the former were so important that they barred certain groups from holding them. For example, regular officials who had transferred from the lower-ranking clerical service were not allowed to hold pure offices. An examination of the list of offices that Quan Deyu held reveals that he served his entire career in pure posts. Moreover, his official duties often brought him into contact with the Emperor. For example, for nine years beginning in 794, regardless of the offices he nominally held, Quan was mostly engaged in the arduous task of drafting imperial proclamations. The sources suggest that Quan was particularly successful at this task; a number of the sources remark on how exceptional his long tenure was. For several years, Quan actually handled the drafting alone, a task which usually required at least three officials. Even Emperor Dezong (r. 780–805) recognized the strain on Quan, but in response to Quan's request that the Emperor fill drafting vacancies, the Emperor pointed out that the importance of the work made it difficult to find qualified men. While such an answer did not lighten Quan's workload, the Emperor's implied compliment tells us much about the esteem Quan enjoyed.

Although Quan himself did not enter the bureaucracy via the examinations, his intellectual credentials were widely recognized at the time. He was broadly learned and an incisive thinker. That he was respected as an intellectual is clear from his successive appointments as an examiner for the civil service examinations. Between 797 and 807, he set questions for a variety of examinations. These included the *jinshi* examination, the "illuminating the Classics" examination, and Daoist examinations. Furthermore, he actually acted as Chief Examiner in 802, 803, and 805. Thus, Quan had a good deal of credibility with two important segments of the government elite, those who entered, as he had done, on the basis of family service and those who had entered via the examinations. This was not simply a bureaucratic issue. When intellectuals debated the best way to solve the dynasty's problems during this period, they invariably focused on the importance of getting the right men into government service. Quan's close association with the examinations made him an authority on recruiting good men. His success in choosing good men only strengthened this reputation. A succession of future grand counselors received their degrees during his tenure as Examiner, and his fame for "getting men" continued into the subsequent Song period.

The description of the Tang bureaucracy and Quan's position in it should not be taken to suggest that government operated smoothly in the late eighth and early ninth centuries. The An Lushan rebellion had shattered the institutions of the dynasty, and the post-rebellion period witnessed a continuous, albeit ultimately unsuccessful, battle to restore political and social stability. Although a full account of the challenges facing the imperial court during this period is well beyond the scope of this short chapter, some familiarity with the situation will illuminate Quan Deyu's political views.

By far the most serious problem confronting the central government was the decline in its power relative to the provinces after the rebellion. The effort to suppress the rebellion required two extraordinary measures. First, to shore up loyal regions and mobilize resources for the dynasty's defense, the court granted wide autonomy to provincial governors over their jurisdictions. Second, the court weakened the rebellion by encouraging defections from within its ranks. It did this by granting a number of generals within the rebellion autonomous provincial governorships in return for their assistance in defeating the remaining rebels. It proved exceedingly difficult to take back the authority these governors had been granted. The result was that much of the northeast remained outside court control with military commanders running essentially independent political administrations and commands—frequently passing them from father to son. Elsewhere, essentially loyal governors nevertheless took the opportunity to increase their personal power and wealth.

The development of provincial autonomy after the rebellion directly affected the way the empire was governed. The provincial administrations became an intervening level authority between the capital and local society. As such, they exercised a great deal of power, especially in financial matters. The provincial administrations filled an important vacuum. Even before the rebellion, the Tang taxation system had grown inefficient. Early Tang taxation was based on individual tax assessments: every person in the empire (except those with tax exemptions) was assessed for three types of taxes (grain, cloth, and labor service). Such a system required carefully maintained population registers. In an empire with a population in excess of 50 million, this was a tall order even in the best of times. By the eighth century, there was a generally recognized problem with an under-registration of population. The serious disruption of north China and the flight of many people south, when coupled with the increased autonomy granted to military commands, completely undermined the Tang revenue system. The dynasty therefore had to abandon its traditional system and adopt a new system that based taxation on property value rather than individuals. Moreover, it had to rely on provincial administrations to collect its taxes. Not every provincial governor enthusiastically forwarded the collection to the capital.

To supplement the reduced resources from the regular taxation system, the dynasty created new institutions that competed with the regular bureaucracy and were often staffed by men who specialized in financial affairs. The surviving records from this period reveal the emperors' deep concern with finances and their willingness to use questionable means to secure needed funds. The result was a rift: on the one hand were bureaucrats who believed that the traditional bureaucratic structure with its emphasis on proper procedure and generalist officials offered the best means to restore dynastic authority. On the other were those who felt that circumstances required new institutions and a greater emphasis on financial expertise.

The rebellion also upset the balance between military power and civil authority. Although in theory the civil authority represented by the central government bureaucracy still held overall authority, the reality was that military officials often operated with minimal oversight. The reliance on powerful military figures to control the various provincial commands also placed enormous power in the hands of officials with concurrent civil and military authority. There was great suspicion of such men among regular officials because of the threat they posed to the central government.

Quan's successful career and proximity to the court gave him the opportunity and authority to address these pressing issues. We can see his distaste for the extraordinary financial arrangements undertaken by the Emperor Dezong early in the second stage of his career. In 793, while still in the relatively low-ranking post of Rectifier of Omissions, Quan submitted two memorials to the throne concerning the operation of one of the financial organs that had undergone the most change since the rebellion. The Department of Public Revenue had originally been a subordinate office of the Ministry of Finance, but in the chaos of the late eighth century, it gradually superseded the ministry and increased its control over most aspects of finance in north China. As a result, it was staffed by officials with financial expertise who were committed to raising as much revenue as possible from a variety of sources. In 792, an official named Pei Yanling (728–796) was appointed head of the department. Pei's willingness to use methods of questionable legitimacy in raising revenue for the emperor drew the ire of many prominent officials. Among other dubious dealings, Pei manipulated account books, shifted funds from public treasuries to the emperor's personal treasury, and authorized the confiscation of goods from the populace. Quan's memorials took particular aim at the unsavory nature of Pei's operation. He implied that one of the most important problems with Pei's conduct in office was the way his actions took place beyond the scrutiny of the regular bureaucracy. Of course, Quan was indicting what he saw as the venality of a specific official, but, in the context of administrative reorganization and fiscal crisis, his criticism must also be interpreted as an objection to the irregular financial measures employed by the court.

During this period, Quan also made clear his concern over the power of the provincial governors. On a number of occasions he advised the emperor to find ways to control or reduce the power of individual governors. The clearest example took place in 810 C.E. Soon after Quan became Grand Counselor, the wealthy and powerful provincial governor Wang E (740–815) came to pay his respects at court. Wang had held a number of high-level provincial commands and been a generally loyal figure. He was not, however, part of the educated elite. Although he had studied the *Spring and Autumn Annals*, one of the Five Classics, he was mocked for claiming that he was a classical scholar (*ru*). Nevertheless, he did have powerful friends in the capital who proposed to the emperor that Wang be granted the title of Grand Counselor in addition to his military command. Quan objected strongly, and offered the following argument to Emperor Xianzong (r. 805–820) in a memorial preserved in the old Tang history:

> The matters of the Grand Counselor are not something one gets in the normal course of promotions. Those who during this dynasty have been Prime Ministers serving in military commands have had great loyalty and great merit. Since the Dali reign period (767–779), there have been cases when there was no choice but to grant the title to men who were recalcitrant and difficult to control. Yet, today, Wang E has no great loyalty or merit. Furthermore, it is not a time for indulgence. Though one wants to use this title, actually I fear that it is not permissible.

Quan's comments suggest that he was concerned with two related issues. First was the excessive accumulation of power in the hands of the military governor. As noted above, much had been ceded to the military governors in the provinces during the previous half-century. Quan balked at a needless concession. Second, Quan wished to preserve the prerogatives of the central government. The title of Grand Counselor was not simply an empty title; it signified significant contributions to the dynasty and therefore should not be cheapened by granting it to someone like Wang E. Wang did eventually receive the title in 814, but Quan and his allies carried the day in 810.

One year earlier Quan had recognized how complex the reassertion of central power over the provinces was, but he continued to reveal his distrust of governors with only military credentials. In the fourth month of 809, he submitted a memorial to the throne suggesting that the emperor take advantage of the death of a military governor's father to appoint a replacement (since the governor would go into a lengthy mourning). In the course of his argument, he drew a strong contrast between the father who had passed the *jinshi* examination, and the son who had simply risen through the military ranks. Thus, Quan, the product of a newly prominent bureaucratic family, explicitly sought to defend the interests of the regular, central bureaucracy against the incursions of those without the proper qualifications.

Despite his defense of the imperial center, Quan frequently stressed the concomitant moral responsibilities of the emperor. For example, in 811, Emperor Xianzong asked his Grand Counselors whether priority should be given to leniency or harshness in government. Quan responded by pointing out that, historically, harsh regimes were short-lived and lenient ones flourished. This resulted from the bond created by benevolent government between the ruling family and the minds of the people. Three months later a notorious legal case provided Quan with the opportunity to elaborate on his views of the emperor's responsibility in guiding the population. In the fifth month, two Grain Transport Commissioners were caught committing large-scale embezzlement. Emperor Xianzong initially waived the death penalty and instead exiled them to the far south. Unfortunately for the criminals, he apparently reconsidered the sentence soon thereafter and sent agents to intercept them on the road with orders for them to commit suicide. Although Quan admitted that the severity of their crime warranted the death penalty, he worried about the mixed signals sent by the Emperor. The law, Quan argued, was a means of instructing the people. By saying one thing and doing another, Emperor Xianzong had confused the people.

Nevertheless, Quan was not simply a moralistic idealist. He backed up his moral arguments with a realistic appraisal of contemporary conditions. We have already seen how Quan could distinguish among the situations in the different autonomous commands. One additional example will have to suffice to demonstrate the point. In 803, Quan submitted a memorial calling for tax relief after a severe drought. The memorial, while calling for a traditional remedy, revealed Quan's understanding of larger economic trends. It pointed out that the tax burden on the population was actually rising because of a persistent deflation that made paying taxes more expensive.

Thus far, we have only considered Quan's political career. Quan's stature went well beyond his official rank. He was one of the towering intellectuals of his day and actively pursued learning in most of the subjects that interested medieval Chinese scholars. He crafted a coherent defense of literary culture that recognized the danger of excessive decadence (which some had suggested was responsible for the political troubles of the eighth century) but that also demonstrated the legitimacy of traditional literary pursuits. His views proved very attractive to educated men of the time. His credibility here was doubtless enhanced by his own attractive literary style. The list of people for whom he composed commemorative texts is a veritable who's who of Tang elite society. It includes not only former grand counselors, such as Du You (735–812), but also respected religious figures, such as the famous Taoist Wu Yun (d. 778) and the Chan master Mazu Daoyi (709–788).

Quan did not see literary activity as simply an art form. He believed that it taught one how to respond to different situations, a skill that was essential in every aspect of life, and especially in government service. This was a quality that he termed "completeness." This search for completeness encouraged him to pursue numerous other subjects. Quan actively pursued an interest in what might be called interior questions. His explorations of the way moral men should conduct themselves found expression in the essays he wrote on human nature (*xing*) and destiny (*ming*) that proved influential and helped draw greater attention to the text of the *Doctrine of the Mean*, a chapter of the *Book of Rites* that would become a central text of the Neo-Confucian school during the subsequent Song dynasty. He investigated medieval China's other great traditions as well. We know, for example, that Quan practiced Taoist and Buddhist forms of self-cultivation. Ultimately, Quan saw both private cultivation and public service as necessary to a complete life and refused to separate moral, cultural, and political accomplishments.

STAGE THREE: THE FINAL YEARS OF QUAN'S CAREER, 813–818

Quan Deyu held the office of Grand Counselor for just over two years, but his tenure in that office was not entirely satisfying. Despite the gradual reinvigoration of the court during these years, great challenges continued to confront the dynasty. His experience as a Grand Counselor illustrates two enduring themes in the political history of the Tang period. The nature of the post itself created problems for the grand counselors. There was generally more than one in that office. The counselors were thus rarely in a position to act unilaterally. Astute emperors, such as Xianzong, made careful use of this to maintain their control over the bureaucracy. This maneuver could engender problems, however, since emperors could be confronted with irreconcilable disagreements among their key advisers.

Rivalry among the grand counselors was a natural tendency in this situation, and it often exacerbated political differences, thereby complicating decision-making. The Tang government was plagued in the ninth century with the problem of factionalism. Research on factionalism has shown that it was an exceedingly complex phenomenon that cannot easily be correlated with policy disputes, social background, or personality clashes. Although it was several decades before the most devastating factional struggles seized the government, already in the second decade of the century we can see the mix of personalities and politics creating tension within the highest echelons of the government.

Quan Deyu's tenure as a grand counselor ultimately foundered on this clash of bureaucratic structure and factionalism. Xianzong was an active emperor and promoted officials with strong opinions. In 813, he summoned an official named Li Jifu (758–814) to be a grand counselor. Unfortunately, Li had serious differences with Grand Counselor Li Jiang (764–830). The result was the ninth-century version of governmental gridlock as the two Lis could not agree on policy proposals. The situation was so bad that the two grand counselors actually argued in the presence of the Emperor. For his part, Quan Deyu, a fellow grand counselor, was mocked because of his inability to resolve the situation. He therefore bowed to pressure and resigned as Grand Counselor, and resumed his duties as Minister of Rites.

His departure from the Grand Counselorship did not remove him from important and prestigious positions. It did, however, give him his first meaningful responsibility outside the capital. In the seventh month of 813, he was appointed Governor of Luoyang, the Tang secondary capital. There he earned a reputation for good governance. The next year he returned to the capital as Minister in the Court of Imperial Sacrifices, a post he held until 815, when he was appointed Minister of Justice. Finally, his last appointment came in the eleventh month of 816 when he was appointed Military Commissioner of the Shannan West military command (in modern Shaanxi and Sichuan provinces). Thus, at the end of his career, he fulfilled the ideal that he had argued for earlier: the administration of a provincial command by a highly educated civil official. His career ended a little over a year and a half later in the eighth month of 818. He fell ill at his post and died during the journey back to the capital.

CONCLUSION

This brief account of Quan Deyu's life has emphasized his public career. This is not because we lack sources to document his personal life. His writings, for example, reveal a sensitive individual with an ability to engage in self-deprecating humor. Instead, Quan's political career has been the focus because it affords us a glimpse of two important phenomena. First, it reveals the kinds of pressures and challenges that Tang officials faced as they attempted to return the empire to order and unity in the early ninth century. Second, it reveals how the Tang system incorporated some less prominent families into the national ruling class. The result, at least in the instance of Quan Deyu, was the creation of a passionate defender of the interests of the dynasty.

SUGGESTED READINGS

Barrett, Timothy. *Li Ao: Buddhist, Taoist, or Neo-Confucian?* Oxford, 1992.

Bol, Peter K. *This Culture of Ours: Intellectual Transitions in T'ang and Sung China*. Stanford, 1992.

Ebrey, Patricia. *The Aristocratic Families of Early Imperial China: A Case Study of the Po-ling Ts'ui Family*. Cambridge, MA, 1978.

Johnson, David. *Medieval Chinese Oligarchy*. Boulder, Colo., 1977.

McMullen, David. *State and Scholars in T'ang China*. Cambridge, England, 1988.

Twitchett, Denis, ed. *Cambridge History of China*, Volume 3: *Sui and T'ang China, 589–906, Part 1*. Cambridge, England, 1979.

Wright, Arthur F., and Denis Twitchett, eds. *Perspectives on the T'ang*. New Haven, 1973.

CHAPTER 6

Yue Fei

1103–1141

Robert W. Foster

The rise of the Song dynasty marks the transition from the Middle Period to the Late Imperial age in China. The changes involved not only the reconfiguration of the imperial state, with the establishment of the Confucian examination system as the principal mechanism for recruitment of officials, but also the redefinition of the social and political elite as one based on learning rather than aristocratic pedigree. The Song was a time of broad economic and intellectual change as well, with China becoming more commercialized, and with new forms of Confucian thought assuming prominence. Finally, it was a period where China had to cope with a complex and dynamic international environment, as the great age of conquest dynasties began, with non-Chinese peoples successively seizing control of larger and larger portions of Chinese territory.

Tensions abounded within the social and political life of Song China. Robert Foster, assistant professor of East Asian history and coordinator of Asian studies at Berea College, Kentucky, uses the tragic story of Yue Fei to illuminate some of the most significant polarities and antagonisms of the cataclysmic years when northern China was taken over by the Jurchen people, and the Song court was forced to flee south for survival. These tensions involve conflicts of interest between civil officials and military leaders, the psychological and political implications of military weakness for the remnant Southern Song dynasty after 1127, and the intricacies of court politics in a time of instability and turmoil.

One day around the year 1134, Yue Fei, the youngest and most successful military commander of the Song dynasty, ascended a pavilion in the town of Jiangzhou and looked out upon the Yangtze River and the lands to the north. The view inspired him to write the poem, "River of Red":

In anger my hair stands in my helmet.
Leaning on the railing as the gusting rain stops,
I gaze upward, looking to Heaven, loudly roaring my intense feelings.
Thirty years' accomplishments like dust and dirt.
I traveled eight thousand *li* with the clouds and the moon.

Never waiting never resting has whitened this young head,
My vain despair is complete.
The shame of the Jingkang period has not yet been wiped away.
When will this subject's anger be erased?
Let me drive a war-chariot to trample them at Helan Mountain.
My ambition is to feast on barbarian flesh when hungry,
And, with light conversation, drink the blood of the Huns.
Let me try again, I will recover our old lands,
Then report to the emperor.

Just a few years later, in the twelfth month of 1141, Yue Fei was executed in his prison cell, out of the public gaze. Why would the Song dynasty condone, or even actively seek, the death of one of the men most responsible for the survival and restoration of the Zhao family as emperors of China? To understand this, one must consider not only the tumultuous times in which Yue Fei lived and thrived but also the larger military, political, and social context of the Song dynasty.

Prior to Yue Fei's birth in 1103, the Song dynasty had developed a pattern of behavior that was to shape the treatment Yue Fei received as a general in the cause of the dynasty. Zhao Kuangyin had founded the Song through a bloody usurpation of the throne held by the young boy under whose father Zhao had been a loyal general. At this time, in 960, China was a divided polity. The collapse of the Tang in 907 led to the rise of regional powers, none of which could unify what had been the imperial boundaries. This fifty-three-year period preceding the Song has been aptly termed the Five Dynasties, due to the fragmented nature and mercurial fortunes of the groups that rose to power. General Zhao's actions were not unique to the period: other generals had usurped authority from their rulers. Once enthroned with the reign-title Song Taizu, however, he took steps to limit the power of the military. This policy was firmly entrenched by his successor, Song Taizong, who instituted the policy of recruiting civil officials from the social group known as the *shidafu*, men whose power was, at this point, based on culture rather than politics. The *shidafu* were scholars steeped in the philosophical and literary traditions of China's past. The political match proved a sound one. The Zhao family found a group without military power of its own who could serve the interests of the dynasty, while the *shidafu* achieved social and political power through their association with the royal family.[1] The generals who had served with and supported Zhao Kuangyin's quest for power were promoted to positions without direct control of the military, and military officers were placed under the command of the civil officials.

The political position of the Song also had direct bearing on the development of Yue Fei's career. In 1103, when Yue Fei was born into a farming family in Tangyin County (near modern Anyang), the Song could claim to be the heir of previous Chinese dynasties that had controlled the Central Plains, but it could not claim preeminence in East Asia. After the collapse of the Tang Empire in the aftermath of the An Lushan rebellion, the non-Han Chinese peoples of Inner and East Asia formed their own dynasties as powers independent of Han Chinese overlords. Song was founded in a multistate world. By the twelfth century, the Song had reached a tenuous accommodation with the Khitan people's Liao dynasty to the north and the Tanggut's Xi Xia dynasty to the northwest. This did not mean that the Song stopped there. When another northern ethnic group, the Jurchens, arose in Manchuria and founded their own Jin dynasty, independent of the Liao, the Song court saw this as an opportunity to regain the northern Yan-Yun territories (around present-day Beijing) that were under Liao control. With an alliance formed between Song and Jin, the two dynasties attacked the Liao in 1122.

When the call went out for recruits to fill the ranks of the Song armies marching north, Yue Fei was a young man interested in the military arts, but steeped in Confucian traditions of loyalty and virtuous conduct as well. His family, though tenant farmers, had been independent landowners until a flood destroyed their village in 1103, shortly after Yue Fei's birth. The family also had a tradition of valuing education. Yue Fei's fourth-generation ancestor, Yue Huan, had been a low-level functionary, but not a full member of the civil service ranks. Though Huan's descendants had not followed his path of official service, the family was probably in the upper ranks of the peasantry, since Yue Fei did receive an education. Yet Yue Fei chose not to pursue a career that drew upon his literacy. Instead, he learned the martial arts from a local man and then volunteered for military service when the call went out in 1122. This was an interesting choice, because the military was often—and for good reason—viewed with disdain. Given the Song founding fathers' inclination to diminish the status of the military, it attracted those who had few other social outlets and were often assumed to have little potential. A popular saying ran, "Don't use good men as soldiers, don't use good iron to make nails." Furthermore, the armies were often built upon personal loyalties, rather than patriotism and sense of duty. This was exacerbated by the dynasty's policy of co-opting the surrender of bandit gangs by offering them postings within the official troops.

The 1122 campaign against the Liao was successful insofar as it diminished Liao's power; however, the Song military leadership under the eunuch Tong Guan proved to be inept. Though Yue Fei's unit made it to sighting distance of the city walls of Yanjing, the Song troops were unable to accomplish their goal of recapturing the area. They had to appeal to their Jurchen allies for support. Consequently, when peace was established, the Jurchens decided to claim the area for themselves. The poor showing on the part of the Song forces may also have given the Jurchen Jin pause to consider future plans, for in 1125, the Jin launched a pincer attack on the Song's northern territories. After successful campaigns in the north, the Jin temporarily withdrew early in 1126, after the Song agreed to pay the Jin annually 300,000 taels of silver, 300,000 bolts of cloth, and 1 million strings of cash over a period of 180 years.[2] However, the war was not over. In 1127, the two prongs of the renewed pincer attack were able to meet at their goal of Kaifeng, the Song capital. There the Jurchens seized the former emperor Huizong, the current emperor Qinzong, and many members of the imperial family and court, and transported them to the north. This would have spelled the end of the Song, except that an imperial scion, the Prince of Kang, was in the field leading the Song forces south of Kaifeng. The prince retreated south, and was enthroned as the next emperor, Gaozong. The Jin had, in the meantime, established the first of two puppet states that would serve as buffers between Jin and Song. The first, known as the State of Chu, was short-lived, but the State of Qi, led by the former Song official Liu Yü, endured until 1139.

After the collapse of the Song attack on Liao in 1122, Yue Fei withdrew from the military to mourn the passing of his father that same year. He reappeared two years later, in 1124, as a bodyguard for the Han family, from whom the Yues rented their land. But with the Jin invasion of 1125, Yue Fei signed up for his second tour of duty. Though still a minor officer, now within the army commanded by Zhang Suo, Yue Fei acquitted himself well in the fight against the Jin invasion. He was promoted and used the opportunity to memorialize the emperor, advocating a stronger militant position. It was presumptuous for such a low-level officer to directly memorialize the throne, and his rewards were rescinded.[3] Yue Fei, however, continued to serve under Zhang Suo's command. Even when Gaozong announced an "imperial tour" of the southeast in the seventh month of 1127, which effectively removed the court from close proximity to the battle lines, Yue Fei continued to fight as a guerrilla north of the Yellow River. When Zhang Suo was cashiered, Yue initially struck out on his own. (One scholar even suggests that Yue became another local bandit, but this seems unlikely given Yue's distaste for bandits.)[4] However, he eventually joined the forces under Zong Ze. The early months of 1128 found Yue Fei fighting around Kaifeng, which Zong Ze's forces lost, recaptured, and lost again. Zong Ze, like Yue Fei, strongly believed in fighting to regain the north.) Shortly after the second loss of Kaifeng, Zong Ze became ill and summoned his commanders to his bedside. There he told them, "If you are not victorious, you should be the first to die." As his officers left the room, Zong Ze shouted three times, "Cross the river!" and then died.[5]

Unfortunately for the Song, and frustratingly for Yue Fei, Du Chong was selected as Zong Ze's replacement. Du Chong did not display the same military ardor as Zong Ze had. As Yue Fei fought north of the Yellow River late in 1128, a series of setbacks afflicted the Song cause. Li Cheng, who had been a guerrilla fighter for the Song, surrendered to the Jin, which immediately turned its troops against the Song. In a similar vein, Liu Yü, who had been holding the strategic city of Jinan in Shandong, surrendered the city in the twelfth month. The Jin then placed Liu upon the throne of the State of Qi, the second puppet-buffer state created by the Jin. These events gave Jin the momentum to press the attack on Song early in 1129. Just prior to this invasion, Du Chong ordered Yue Fei and his detachment to attack two other groups within Du Chong's command. These two groups were former bandit gangs that Zong Ze had been able to co-opt, but they had drifted back into brigandage after Zong's death. Though they had come back into the army when Du Chong gained command, he still did not trust them. The former bandits were defeated and scattered in the attack, but this action also reduced the number of troops defending the capital when the Jin attack came. Du Chong"s response was to abandon Kaifeng and Shandong to the Jin and retreat to Jiankang, a strategic city on the southern bank of the Yangtze. To help cover his retreat, Du Chong ordered the diversion of the Yellow River into the channel of the Huai River, shifting the river's flow from north of the Shandong peninsula to its south. The flooding devastated the areas along the Huai.

The repercussions of these successive disasters were strong at the Song court. In the third month of 1129, while the leading generals were holding the defensive line to the north, two discontented military officials decided to take matters into their own hands. Miao Fu and Liu Zhengyan, stationed at the temporary palace in Hangzhou, organized a coup against Gaozong and, more particularly, Wang Yuan, head of the Bureau of Military Affairs. Miao Fu and Liu Zhengyan blamed Wang Yuan for the Song's military losses and for having pared their rewards from these battles. They killed Wang and forced a trapped Gaozong to abdicate in favor of his infant son, with the Longwu Dowager Empress serving as regent. However, the Song's top generals (Han Shizhong, Liu Guangshi, and Zhang Zun) refused to recognize the coup. When they sent detachments to Hangzhou, the Empress Dowager abdicated in favor of Gaozong at the beginning of the next month. Though the coup had been foiled, it had a profound impact upon the court. From 1129 forward, military officials were not allowed to participate in policy discussions at court, and the communications between civil and military officials were closely monitored for signs of treachery. Gaozong himself was distraught by the attempt to supplant him, and, as one historian put it, it had increased "to an almost morbid level the Emperor's craving for marks and signs of subordination in the generals."[6] The incident also increased Gaozong's suspicion of anyone who pressed him to name an heir apparent after the death of his only son four months later.

In the face of these events, Yue Fei continually urged Du Chong to act. In the winter of 1129, as the Jin forces attempted to cross the Yangtze near Jiankang, Yue Fei tearfully pleaded with Du Chong to act: "A powerful enemy is nearby in Huai-nan looking down upon the Yangtze with ample resources. There is no more critical time to be nursing our vengeance. But you sir spend all your days resting at ease and not concerning yourself with military affairs. . . . If the generals do not obey orders and Jinling is lost, will you be able to lie back again on your high pillow here? Even if I sacrificed my lone army, it would not be enough to make things up to the state."[7] When he learned of the Jin preparations to cross the Yangtze, Du Chong deputed Chen Cui to lead 20,000 men to thwart the crossing. Yue Fei's men were among them. The defense of the southern bank held, until one of the other subcommanders began to retreat unexpectedly. This move threw the defense into chaos; Chen Cui was killed, leaving Yue Fei to rally the remaining troops. The next day he counterattacked, inflicting heavy casualties on the Jin troops, but he could not force them back. At the end of the day, the troops were on the verge of disintegrating, when Yue Fei addressed them:

> We have been treated with great generosity by the state. We ought to repay it with our loyalty. If we achieve merit, our fame will be recorded so that even if we die it will not be erased. But if we submit and are taken prisoner, or flee and turn brigand merely to save our lives, when we die our names will be lost in oblivion. Is this what you want? Jiankang is on the left side of the river on defensible terrain. If the Tartar brigands occupy it, what will be left to maintain the state? Today's issue permits no other choice. Anyone who goes out this gate will be beheaded.[8]

Even with this exhortation and warning, scattered remnants of the army turned to banditry. Those who remained, however, became the core of officers in Yue Fei's troops, men who were disciplined and loyal to him. They were central to the most successful army in the empire. When asked how he maintained discipline among his troops in a time when desertion and mutiny were not uncommon, Yue Fei answered, "Benevolence, wisdom, honesty, bravery, and severity; without each one, it would not be possible." It is interesting to note that Yue Fei combined the martial virtues of bravery and severity with the Confucian virtues of benevolence, wisdom, and honesty. His men responded to his leadership. Yet this bond between Yue Fei and his men would also fuel the suspicions and fears of the court and influence the decision to execute him. Yue Fei and his men retreated to Maoshan, where they set up a base to harass the flanks of the invading Jin. In the meantime, Du Chong, disheartened by Jin's successes, boarded a boat with most of the regional treasury and crossed to the north bank to surrender to the Jin.

Like Yue Fei, the rest of the Song forces fell back from the invaders. The eastern prong of the Jin attack pressed farther south, chasing Gaozong out of the temporary capital at Hangzhou. The Jin army pursued him to the port city of Changzhou, where, early in 1130, he took ship and sailed to Wenzhou, about 200 kilometers farther south. By this time, the Jin commander, Wu Zhu, began to pull his troops back, perhaps fearing to overextend his supply lines while loyalist groups like Yue Fei's continued to raid Jin encampments successfully. By the second month, the Jin had pulled back from Hangzhou and begun to retreat to the northern side of the Yangtze.

With the withdrawal of Jin troops, the Song embarked upon an effort to "first pacify the internal to resist the external." As often seen in later Chinese history, the government stressed that Chinese rebels and bandits were "diseases of the vital organs," while foreign threats were "diseases of the extremities." The social and political chaos that had beset China since the Jin invasions of the mid-1120s had provided fertile ground for groups opposing imperial authority. Some groups attempted to establish independent kingdoms, while others merely looted with impunity, never seeking administrative control over the areas they plundered. Many of these groups were comprised of military or local militia units that had deserted, but the economic instability of the period also forced people to join these groups when no other recourse for survival was available. Taxes had risen since 1126, because the government needed to fund the campaigns after losing much of its tax base when the Jin seized the north. At the same time, the invasions sparked mass movements of refugees that strained food supplies and increased the competition for earning a livelihood in the south. These factors led to inflation, as scarce goods became more expensive. Until the economic and social situation stabilized and the government was able to provide a milieu conducive to transporting goods, life in some areas became quite harsh. Recognizing that some banditry was less a consequence of greed and more a product of adverse social conditions, the Song government frequently attempted first to persuade rebels and bandits to surrender peacefully and receive full pardons. This policy was not always successful. As Yue Fei wrote in one memorial, "Every year Your Majesty often commands offers for amnesty. Thus when bandits are strong they are extremely vicious, but when their strength has failed, they accept amnesty. If we do not plan to exterminate even more, their swarming bands will never be completely eliminated."[9]

While Yue Fei was harassing the Jin retreat in the east, civil unrest gripped the area around Lake Dongting in central China. The area was strategically important because it covered the western flank of the Song, providing access to the Sichuan basin. The source of the unrest stemmed from a local strongman and sorcerer named Zhong Xiang, who professed an ability to heal illness and began to attract a large following. In the spring of 1130, he formed his followers into the "Faithful and Virtuous People's Force," proclaiming himself the Great Sage of Heaven. He then led his force to strike down symbols and representatives of authority: government administrative buildings, marketplaces, and temples were burned; gentry, monks, and government clerks were attacked and killed. He declared himself King of Chu and began to set up his own administration. Kong Yanzhou, a roving bandit, who occasionally served the Song, crushed Zhong's rebellion. Kong Yanzhou then allowed his men to plunder towns that had resisted his forces or that he suspected of having helped Zhong Xiang's rebels. The result of his campaign against Zhong may have simply made the local situation worse. As one local recorded after their battles, "Only one in a hundred households remained; provincial cities were razed, commerce and communications cut, taxes were not received, and only a few poor souls were left in the towns. There were no city walls in any direction, not a single coin or a kernel of grain in the storehouses."[10]

Zhong Xiang's death did not stabilize the region. One of his commanders, Yang Yao, had survived the confrontation with Kong Yanzhou's forces and he also had Zhong Xiang's young heir apparent in his custody. Yang Yao fled out into the marshes of Lake Dongting, causing some confusion about how to deal with him. Government administrative units were based upon land surveys. Bodies of water were not apportioned to administrative units. Hence, to a certain extent, those who lived out on the lake's marshes were beyond the law.[11] Yang Yao and his bandits did not have the same dynastic pretensions as Zhong Xiang, choosing instead to live off the towns and fishermen as pirates. Since the lake did not fall under a clear administrative jurisdiction, it was not until the government recognized the potential threat of the bandits that a concerted effort was made to eliminate them.

Early in the campaign, the official in charge hit upon the idea of using human-powered paddle wheelers against Yang Yao's pirates. Unfortunately for this official, he was defeated in his first battle employing these special boats, and Yang Yao captured the carpenter who designed them. Yang then put the carpenter to work, so that by 1135, Yang had a fleet of several hundred boats, including a number of large paddle wheelers. These had multistory towers, carried several hundred men, and some were capable of using pulleys and booms to drop huge rocks onto the decks of attacking ships.

Yue Fei was given the task of putting an end to Yang Yao's banditry when rumors began to circulate that Yang Yao was negotiating a joint campaign with Li Cheng, another former bandit now serving as a general in the armies of the State of Qi. In the third month of 1134, Yue Fei was given authorization to move against Li Cheng in the north and then turn south to deal with Yang Yao. When Yue Fei's troops engaged Li's outside Xiangzhou, Yue Fei noted a fatal flaw in the Qi troops' disposition: "Infantry take advantage of difficult terrain, while cavalry have the advantage on flat, open ground. Li Cheng has deployed his cavalry on the left flank along the riverbank, and deployed his infantry on the right, on level ground. Though he has 100,000 men, what use are they?"[12] Yue Fei consequently sent his infantry armed with pikes against Li Cheng's cavalry that was hemmed in by the river, while deploying his cavalry against the infantry on the flat ground. The outcome was as Yue Fei had predicted: Li Cheng's infantry was routed, and many of his cavalrymen drowned in the river when they could not break through the pikemen. After being defeated at Xiangzhou and a series of successive battles, Li fled north. Yue Fei wrote to the emperor asking permission to continue the pursuit. "The Jin love only their families and wealth," he wrote. "They have become conceited and lazy. Liu Yü is a usurper, so the people have never forgotten Song. If we struck directly into the Central Plain with 200,000 crack troops, we could restore the old boundaries and make them truly strong."[13] The court rejected the invasion plan, not wanting operations against the puppet State of Qi to provoke a Jin response. Yue Fei then turned south to deal with Yang Yao.

He arrived at Lake Dongting in the fourth month of 1135 and, despite his previous advocacy for strong action against bandits, began by sending pacification commissioners offering amnesty into the bandit areas. One bandit who accepted the amnesty, Huang Zuo, received an official rank from Yue Fei, who then sent him back with money and bolts of cloth to win over other bandits. By this means, Yue Fei negotiated the surrender of a few thousand bandits. However, as autumn approached, Yue Fei's immediate superiors received orders to withdraw. Yue Fei boldly asked permission not to withdraw, because he could break the bandits in eight days. Given these eight days, he began by co-opting Yang Qin, one of Yang Yao's top commanders. Yang Qin, too, was given an official title and gifts, and then was sent back to the marshes to bring in even more bandits. With his lieutenants surrendering and his forces dwindling, Yang Yao retreated farther into the lake. To achieve victory, Yue Fei had to draw out Yang Yao's flotilla and then neutralize the superior speed and maneuverability of Yang Yao's paddle wheelers. Yue Fei ordered that the channels and inlets around Yang Yao's base be filled with logs, effectively blocking his avenues of escape. He then had the water covered with floating bundles of grass. Finally, he "selected a shallow area, then sent troops who were good at cursing to harangue the enemy. When the enemy angrily came in pursuit, the grasses and wood clogged [the mechanisms], the ships' wheels were broken, rendering them immobile."[14] Yang Yao then attempted to drown himself, but was captured and beheaded.

Though given promotion and enfeoffed as a duke, Yue Fei asked to be removed from command due to a chronic eye problem. The emperor denied his petition. This was not the first time that Yue Fei had attempted to retire, nor would it be the last. He often submitted requests to retire when he felt that the court had abandoned plans to recapture the north. Though he recognized the need to control banditry and rebellion within Song's shrunken realm, it was also just prior to his quelling of Yang Yao's bandits that Yue Fei had written the poem "River of Red" to vent his frustrations at not being allowed to carry the offensive to the Jin.

Early in 1136, as Yue Fei was preparing to move troops to Xiangzhou to observe enemy activities in the Central Plain better, he received news that his mother had died. He immediately turned over his seals of command and embarked upon the customary period of mourning. Taking her coffin to be buried in Jiangxi, he remained in mourning until the end of the fifth month. He was dissuaded from engaging in the full three-year mourning period by entreaties from Emperor Gaozong to "transform filiality into loyalty" and the advice that regaining the north would be a filial act by gaining honor for his family.[15] Yue Fei used these pleas as a means of getting permission for wider-ranging campaigns in the north. His title was changed to Deputy Commissioner to Proclaim the Imperial Will and Pacify the Frontiers of Hedong, with Hebei circuit also under his command. This effectively gave him administrative prerogatives for campaigning in the north, but Yue Fei had no permission to do so.

While Yue Fei was strenuously seeking Gaozong's sanction of more active campaigning, other members of the court were advising the emperor to pursue a treaty with the Jin. Only with peace, they argued, could Gaozong accomplish the release of the imperial captives taken north in 1127. Foremost among the peace advocates was Qin Gui, who had been an official in Huizong's court in Kaifeng prior to the Jin invasion of 1125. When the Jin forced the surrender of the Song court, Qin Gui had petitioned the Jin to keep Huizong on the throne and swore that he would serve no other ruler, so the Jin transported him, along with many other courtiers, to the north. After being taken to the north with Huizong and Qinzong, Qin Gui was given to the Jurchen lord Da Lai. Da Lai found him to be a man of parts and made him his military adviser and transportation commissioner for the invasions of 1129–30. Qin Gui persuaded Da Lai to allow Qin Gui's wife to accompany the invasion, as was the Jin custom. Upon arriving in the south, Qin and his wife were able to escape from the Jin troops besieging Chuzhou. This story was treated with suspicion by many in the south. Some even accused Qin Gui of being a Jin agent, due to his ardent pursuit of a peace treaty. In his first audience with Gaozong, Qin Gui told him, "If it is desired that the Empire be without crisis it is necessary for the south to stay in the south and the north to stay in the north. Then consultations to discuss peace can be set up."[16] It is no great surprise, then, that Yue Fei and Qin Gui became bitter rivals.

In order to sue for peace successfully, Qin Gui believed he needed to curtail the power of the leading generals. As noted, many of these armies had not developed as official units independent of specific officers. Instead, these armies tended to be accretions of recruits, criminals sentenced to military service, and surrendered bandit groups. Consequently, loyalty and discipline were frequently based upon the personal relationships within the officer corps. In 1137, the Song was dealt a blow by the mishandling of these relationships. Liu Guangshi, one of the leading generals, but also the least successful one, was removed from command of his troops. Qin Gui did not want these troops added to Yue Fei's army, since this would increase Yue Fei's authority. Instead, Qin Gui told Yue Fei to assist the head of the Bureau of Military Affairs, Zhang Jun, in distributing the troops. The problem was that two of Liu Guangshi's top commanders, Wang De and Li Huan, were both former bandits with large personal entourages in the army. When Zhang Jun proposed placing Wang De in command, but subordinating him to a civil official named Lü Zhi, Yue Fei disapproved. He told Zhang Jun, "Clearly Wang De and Li Huan have always been of equal rank. If you suddenly promote one above the other, there will be trouble. Minister Lü is not trained in military affairs. I fear he will not be able to control the army."[17] Yue Fei argued that he was the only one capable of controlling the two men and their followers. There was some merit to his argument, as Yue Fei's troops were known to be the best disciplined in Song. Zhang Jun grew angry at Yue Fei for rejecting each of his suggestions. Ultimately, Zhang Jun implemented his original plan, putting Lü Zhi in command with Wang De in charge of the troops. Yue Fei's assessment proved correct. Li Huan rebelled, killed Lü Zhi, and took 40,000 troops over to the enemy. The loss of such a large body of trained soldiers obviously shook the court and enhanced the persuasive power of pursuing a peace policy.

Added to the betrayal by Li Huan, at the end of 1137, the Jin decided that Liu Yü's State of Qi was not successfully protecting Jin political and military interests. Liu Yü was removed from power, honorably enfeoffed in the north, and Qi was dissolved. Some credit Yue Fei with orchestrating Liu Yü's downfall by selecting a man he knew to be a Jin spy to carry a letter addressed to Liu Yü discussing secret plans for Liu Yü to surrender to the Song. The spy then immediately showed the letter to Wu Zhu, the heir apparent of Jin, who wanted to pursue war with the Song. Wu Zhu then received permission to dissolve Qi. Whether Yue Fei did or did not engineer the break-up of Qi, he did memorialize that Song ought to take advantage of the temporary break in lines of command and invade the north.[18] He received no response from the emperor, who had been officially informed that his father, Emperor Huizong, had died in the north.

During 1138, Song and Jin continually sent embassies to one another to discuss terms for a peace treaty and the delivery of the Huizong's coffin to Song. Yue Fei persistently protested these talks. Perhaps to mollify him when a settlement was reached early in 1139, Yue Fei was promoted again. As before, Yue Fei declined this promotion and used his letter to criticize the peace policy. "The events of today are cause for danger, not for peace; they are lamentable, not laudable. We ought to be instructing soldiers and issuing commands to officers. There are no worries with full preparations. But we cannot discuss achievements and dole out rewards. This invites our enemy's laughter."[19]

Once again, Yue Fei was proven correct. Due to factional purges in Jin, the advocates of peace had been replaced by the prowar faction led by Wu Zhu. Perhaps significantly, Da Lai, the man whom Qin Gui had served during his captivity in Jin, had led the peace faction. Da Lai tried to fight his way south to the Song, but was captured and executed by Wu Zhu in the autumn of 1139. In the fifth month of 1140, the Jin launched a pincer attack on Song avoiding Yue Fei's troops stationed in the center of the Song defenses. Song forces were roundly defeated in many of the initial battles. The emperor called upon Yue Fei to counterattack. By the sixth month, Yue Fei's troops had turned the tide of the invasion and had pushed the front north into Jin territory. Soon they were fighting in the Luoyang region, near the former Song capital of Kaifeng. But the emperor cautioned Yue Fei not to press too far north. Yue Fei's troops took Zhengzhou, between Luoyang and Kaifeng at the end of the sixth month. Morale was high after victory over Wu Zhu in the seventh month. As Yue Fei's troops moved north, a skirmish between advance patrols led to the pursuit of retreating Jin cavalry. Yue Fei saw the chase and wanted to join. According to an account written by his grandson, one of Yue Fei's officers named Huo Jian "grasped [Yue Fei's] horse by the bridle and remonstrated: 'My lord, you are an important official of the state in peace and war. How can you go to battle so lightly protected?' Grandfather whipped Jian's hand and, waving the whip at him, said, 'You would not understand.' He then rushed into the thick of the battle, shooting to his left and right. The morale of his officers increased manifold, not one failing to be a match for a hundred. Their shouts shook the earth and victory was won on the spot."[20] At this point, Yue Fei was optimistic as his troops continued to press the Jin troops. He told his officers, "This time we will kill the foreigners right up to Huanglong fu [in Manchuria] where I'll get good and drunk with you gentlemen."[21] Yue Fei believed it was time to fulfill his vow to Gaozong to forswear drinking until the north was regained.

At this point the emperor sent congratulations and called upon Yue Fei to come to court once the operations solidifying the position were complete. Yue Fei found this a difficult order to accept, given that Wu Zhu was pulling all Jin noncombatants back to the northern side of the Yellow River. Yue Fei memorialized that his lieutenant Liang Xing "and others have crossed the Yellow River. The people long to submit to the court. The Jin are consistently being defeated. Wu Zhu and others are ordering the old and young to go north. This is truly the moment for the Restoration!" This was not merely Yue Fei's exaggerated assessment of the situation. Wu Zhu attempted to pull his troops together for a counterattack, but could not gather sufficient forces due to the retreat and surrender of many units. He lamented that Jin had never suffered such defeat and demoralization before.[22] Yet the Song court did not take advantage of the victories that Yue Fei was scoring. He was recalled south. In one day he received several copies of the order to withdraw. This must have been truly devastating to him. At the brink of success, he had the choice of disobeying orders and pressing the attack or submitting himself to the emperor's will. Yue Fei ordered his troops to prepare for withdrawal, lamenting "ten years of effort, lost in one morning."[23] When the local populace heard that the Song troops were pulling back, they blocked the road and sent a delegation to plead with Yue Fei. They feared that the Jin would punish them for the aid they gave the Song armies. Yue Fei delayed his retreat five days to provide cover for those civilians who chose to flee to the south; he also recommended that the court grant them farmland that had been deserted during previous campaigns.

This was the last great military campaign of Yue Fei's career. Though called upon to block another Jin invasion early in 1141, the military confrontation with the Jin bogged down into a stalemate. Yue Fei never again received permission to attack Jin. The court decided to reward the three generals who had led the Song armies. Yet the rewards were double-edged. Following the precedent set by the early Song emperors, the generals were given offices within the civil bureaucracy's Bureau of Military Affairs, and were thereby removed from their troops. The other two generals, Han Shizhong and Zhang Jun, both accepted the rewards and promotions gracefully. Yue Fei's continued requests to be allowed to retire were consistently rejected by the emperor. It is unclear whether Gaozong did not want to lose his best general, or if he wanted to make sure that Yue Fei remained where he could be more easily controlled. The emperor ordered that Yue Fei's house in Hangzhou be expanded, befitting the general's service to the empire. While Gaozong seems to have been truly fond of Yue Fei, he was also shrewd enough to recognize that Yue Fei, in office or in retirement, represented a rallying point for irredentists. Qin Gui certainly recognized this and was actively pursuing legal investigations that he hoped would at least lead to Yue Fei's dismissal. Initially, Yue Fei was accused of misappropriation of funds, but no evidence of it could be found. The best case that could be brought against him was that Yue Fei had been late in moving troops during one campaign. But even for this offense, there was contradictory evidence, so no conviction ensued.

However, Qin Gui did find a subordinate of Zhang Xian, one of Yue Fei's most trusted generals, who testified that Zhang Xian and Yue Fei plotted rebellion. On the grounds of this man's deposition, Yue Fei and his eldest son, Yue Yun, were summoned for interrogation. Though his friends urged him not to submit, Yue laughed and turned himself in. As his interrogation began, he tore off his shirt to show the inquisitors his back, upon which had been tattooed the words "repay the nation with utmost loyalty." The investigation could find no evidence of malfeasance. Yue Fei would admit nothing, and no one provided further support for the accusation lodged against him.

Concurrent with the investigation, the Song court had renewed negotiations with Jin for Huizong's coffin. During these talks Jin conveyed their displeasure with Yue Fei. One account relates that Wu Zhu sent a letter to Qin Gui demanding Yue Fei's death as a prerequisite for successful negotiations. Another notes that Wu Zhu expressed his vexation with continued loyalist guerrilla activity in Jin territory. Since Yue Fei had been the most vociferous proponent of supporting the guerrillas, this was interpreted as an indirect statement about Yue Fei being an obstacle to the negotiations. Yet there seems to have been no real connection; the negotiations progressed, resulting in a new treaty in the eleventh month, while the investigation against Yue Fei proved fruitless. Even so, at the end of 1141, when executions were to be carried out, a death warrant was signed for Yue Fei. Not wanting to risk a public execution that might spark public unrest, Qin Gui had Yue Fei killed in his prison cell. Yue Yun and Zhang Xian were publicly executed. When Han Shizhong heard that Qin Gui had condoned the death of his former comrade, he went to Qin Gui and asked what evidence justified such a verdict. Qin

Gui responded that there had been three letters between Zhang Xian and Yue Yun discussing a plot to reunite Yue Fei with his army, but that those letters were not necessary and had been burnt. Han Shizhong incredulously asked, "How can the three words 'were not necessary' mollify the nation?" Once word of Yue Fei's death reached Jin, celebrations were held.

The peace treaty stipulated that the Song would pay an annual tribute of 250,000 taels each of silver and bolts of cloth, and Gaozong accepted lesser status in relation to the Jin ruler. One can imagine Yue Fei's indignation at these terms, particularly after his success against the Jin in 1140. Han Shizhong's estimation of the heavy-handed tactics employed by Qin Gui proved correct. Yue Fei's execution proved a source of criticism of Qin Gui's government. After the treaty of 1141, Qin Gui's position at the court was solidified and he was able to take harsh retaliation against those critical of his handling of Yue Fei and of the peace treaty in general. Some who publicly decried Yue Fei's execution were themselves executed. Disapproving officials were stripped of office and exiled. However, the peace was sustained.

Yue Fei symbolized for many people in Song the struggle of the righteous military man fighting for his homeland against a corrupt, possibly treacherous, civil official. His life and fate are indicative of the strengths and problems inherent in the Song policy of subordinating the military to the civil. On the one hand, there were no successful military coups toppling the Song imperial line. On the other, civil authority bore more weight than military, making it all the more difficult for Yue Fei to convince the court of his policies. During Yue Fei's life, the court and civil officials were probably increasingly convinced of the necessity of ensuring that civil authority had the upper hand as army units deserted to the Jin or became bandits preying upon their fellow countrymen.

The underlying reason for Yue Fei's execution is not clear. Obviously he was a thorn in the side of those promoting peaceful coexistence with Jin. Emperor Gaozong had, for fifteen years, been trying to maintain the Song imperial line, despite being driven from the north and then from successive temporary capitals by the Jin, and despite the attempted coup of 1129. He was haunted by the captivity of his family in the north and actively pursuing war may have led to their execution. This may have been the motivation to rein in Yue Fei at moments when he seemed ready to sweep aside the Jin. Yet after Qin Gui's death, Gaozong posthumously rehabilitated Yue Fei. His body, which had been secretly buried by a sympathetic prison guard to avoid desecration by Qin Gui's clique, was reburied with honors. Over time Yue Fei's spirit has apotheosized into a god of righteousness and a symbol of patriotism for the Chinese. In the temple dedicated to Yue Fei in modern Hangzhou, statues of Qin Gui, his wife, Zhang Jun, and the inquisitor, Moqi Qiao, kneel in bound submission before Yue Fei's grave as eternal punishment for their role in his execution.

NOTES

1. Peter K. Bol, *This Culture of Ours: Intellectual Transitions in T'ang and Sung China* (Stanford, 1992), 52.

2. Herbert Franke, "The Chin Dynasty," *Alien Regimes and Border States, 907– 1368*, vol. 6: *The Cambridge History of China*, ed. D. Twitchett and H. Franke (Cambridge, England, 1994), 229.

3. Edward Harold Kaplan, "Yueh Fei and the Founding of the Southern Song" (Ph.D. dissertation, University of Iowa, 1970), 62–63.

4. Helmut Wilhelm, "From Myth to Myth: The Case of Yueh Fei's Biography," in *Confucianism and Chinese Civilization*, ed. A. F. Wright (Stanford, 1975), 217.

5. Kaplan, "Yueh Fei," 85.

6. Ibid., 101.

7. Ibid., 120.

8. Ibid., 122.

9. Tuo Tuo, *Songshi [The Song Dynastic History]*, 40 vols. (Beijing: Zhonghua shuju, 1977), sec. 365, p. 11380.

10. John W. Haeger, "Between North and South: The Lake Rebellion in Hunan, 1130–1135," in *Journal of Asian Studies* 28, no. 3 (1969): 474–75.

11. Ibid., 470.

12. Tuo, *Songshi*, sec. 365, p. 11382.

13. Ibid.

14. Ibid., sec. 365, p. 11384.

15. Kaplan, "Yueh Fei," 295.

16. Ibid., 156.

17. Tuo, *Songshi*, sec. 365, p. 11387.

18. Ibid., sec. 365, p. 11388.

19. Ibid.

20. Kaplan, "Yueh Fei," 418.

21. Ibid., 431.

22. Tuo, *Songshi*, sec. 365, p. 11390.

23. Ibid., sec. 365, p. 11391.

SUGGESTED READINGS

Bol, Peter K. *This Culture of Ours: Intellectual Transitions in T'ang and Sung China*. Stanford, 1992.

Franke, Herbert. "The Chin Dynasty." In *Alien Regimes and Border States, 907–1368*, edited by D. Twitchett and H. Franke. Vol. 6: *The Cambridge History of China*. Cambridge, England, 1994: 215–320.

Haeger, John W. "Between North and South: The Lake Rebellion in Hunan, 1130–1135." *Journal of Asian Studies* 28, no. 3 (1969): 469–88.

Kaplan, Edward Harold. "Yueh Fei and the Founding of the Southern Song." Ph.D. dissertation, History, University of Iowa, 1970.

Tuo Tuo. *Songshi [The Song Dynastic History]*. 40 vols. Beijing: Zhonghua shuju, 1977.

Wilhelm, Helmut. "From Myth to Myth: The Case of Yueh Fei's Biography." In *Confucianism and Chinese Civilization*, edited by A. F. Wright. Stanford, 1975: 211–26.

CHAPTER 7

Liu Chenweng

Ways of Being a Local Gentleman in Southern Song and Yuan China

ANNE GERRITSEN

In the thirteenth century, East Asia and much of the rest of the Old World were deeply shaken by the rise of the Mongols, a seminomadic Inner Asian people who, led by the charismatic Chinggis (Genghis) Khan, embarked on a campaign of conquest that eventually gave them an empire stretching from the Pacific to Eastern Europe, and from the Euphrates to Siberia. In China the Mongols first destroyed the Jurchen Jin dynasty that had ruled northern China since 1127, and then went on to conquer the Southern Song. The Mongols proclaimed their own dynasty, the Yuan, in 1271, and held all of China for nearly a century until they were driven out by the founder of the Ming dynasty in 1368.

Under Mongol rule, China was governed as an occupied territory. The Mongols feared and mistrusted the indigenous leaders of the Chinese, the literati or shidafu, *who had come to be the ruling class during the Song. Members of this class were now largely excluded from meaningful participation in government, at least in the first half of the Yuan period. Even without the Mongol conquest, though, the ever increasing number of men taking the Confucian examinations during the Song had already begun to generate a surplus of qualified individuals, many of whom could not hope ever to find employment in the ranks of imperial officials.*

Liu Chenweng (1232–1297) was a successful examination candidate, placing third in the imperial examination in 1262, and he did serve briefly in government posts. But his career was disrupted by the Mongol conquest, and he spent much of his life out of official service. Anne Gerritsen, lecturer in the History Department, University of Warwick, England, explores his role as a member of local society in Jiangxi to show how members of the shi *class coped with their enforced withdrawal from official life and how they functioned as public intellectuals under the Mongol regime. Their activities as writers and cultural authorities shaped local society and helped maintain Chinese traditions and identity during times of conflict and uncertainty.*

111

𝒥n the early months of 1297, a sixty-five-year-old man died in his home in Luling in southern China. Only a fortnight earlier he had celebrated the first evening of the lunar new year, and had made a record of the events. His burial just north of Luling was attended by some of his students, and his friends wrote poems and eulogies for him. One of his fellow students was unable to attend the funeral, but visited his grave the next year and described his sense of loss over his companion of forty years.

Who was this man? Who had he been? He was born as Liu Huiming, later became known by the name Liu Chenweng, while his students referred to him as Master Xuqi. His family was rich enough to give Liu an education, but he never made a great career serving the empire as an official. He wrote poetry, practiced calligraphy, and taught students, but none of these pursuits alone brought him lasting fame. His collected writings were lost during the turmoil at the end of the Mongol Yuan dynasty (1271–1368), and during the compilation of the *Siku quanshu*, the eighteenth-century collection of Chinese literary writings, only one-tenth of Liu's original writings were recovered.

So was he a "nobody"? The fact that we still have access to some of his writings more than seven hundred years later and that his portrait still hangs in the school he attended in Luling testify that he was not. What did Liu Chenweng do to make a name for himself, to "be somebody"? To answer that question is the aim of this biography.

LIU'S LIFE AND LEARNING

Liu was born in 1232 in a small village in Luling County, which was culturally and economically the most prominent of the eight counties that made up Ji prefecture (or Jizhou) in southcentral Jiangxi during the Song dynasty. Jizhou was famous throughout the realm for having produced such sons as the learned Ouyang Xiu (1007–72), the high minister Hu Quan (1102–80), and Liu's contemporary Wen Tianxiang (1236–83), who would become the heroic martyr of the anti-Mongol resistance. These and many other famous scholar–officials from Jizhou gave the area its reputation as a center for learning. During the Song dynasty, Jizhou was also the larger area's economic center. It encompassed the very fertile Jitai basin, which produced a vast surplus of rice. Jizhou's central river, the Gan, which flows from southern Jiangxi northward, was in constant use for the transportation of grain, tea, and locally produced luxury goods to other regions. At Jizhou's kilns, fine porcelain was produced and exported to rival the blue and white wares from the Imperial Kilns at Jingdezhen.

In 1241, a new magistrate arrived in Jizhou. His name was Jiang Wanli (1198–1275), and this man from northern Jiangxi would have great influence on the life of Liu Chenweng. Among the new magistrate's first accomplishments was the founding of an academy. The site Jiang chose for this new academy was a long and narrow island in the river Gan, where it flows past the walls of the county seat. White Egret Islet, stretched out in the river next to the town of Luling, was, and is still today, connected to the western riverbank with a bridge. The prefectural school was also located on this island, and here Jiang established his White Egret Islet Academy in 1241. He appointed a famous scholar from Luling as head of the academy, and the nine-year-old Liu was sent there to study. Over the years that followed, Liu continued his studies in Luling, mostly with learned men and gifted poets from Jizhou. The White Egret Academy continued to flourish, even after Jiang Wanli moved to the capital in 1247, and it was known for the personal and informal style of teaching that Jiang had encouraged here.

Liu met Jiang Wanli again many years later, when Liu was in his late twenties. He had married in the meantime and had two sons. Liu came to the capital in 1260 to enroll as a student at the National University, where Jiang held an appointment as chancellor. Jiang became aware of Liu's writings and praised their skill and beauty, even after Jiang had been promoted to the central secretariat. Two years later, the highest examinations in the capital were held, and Liu passed with good results. If it had not been for Liu's outspoken criticism of the reform policies of Jia Sidao (1213–1275), who was Grand Councillor at the time, the emperor might perhaps have ranked him first instead of third in the palace examinations. His personal circumstances prevented him, however, from accepting a position in the capital. His mother had become very ill, and Liu applied for a provincial post, as headmaster of an academy in Ganzhou, farther south in Jiangxi than Jizhou, to be closer to home.

On his way to Ganzhou, Liu stopped in to see Jiang Wanli, who had moved back to Jiangxi. During the decade that followed, Liu's life was closely intertwined with Jiang Wanli's career. In 1264, when Jiang took up the post of military commander in Fujian while serving as magistrate of Fuzhou, Liu moved to Fuzhou and became Jiang's private secretary. When Jiang moved back to the capital in 1265, he invited Liu to come with him and continue as his assistant. Shortly after their relocation to the capital, Jiang was sent on an assignment to Hunan, and Liu returned home to Luling to await Jiang's return for the next several years. He joined Jiang for several months in Jianghuai in 1268, and followed Jiang again to the capital the year after, when Jiang was promoted to chief councillor in 1269. With Jiang Wanli in such an influential position, he might have been able to push his career significantly forward, but Liu Chenweng's mother died at this time, and Liu left the capital to return home for his mother's mourning period. Later, Jiang's fortunes at the capital were badly affected by the continuing rivalry between Jiang and Grand Councillor Jia Sidao, and Jiang was forced to leave the capital to take up a provincial post. Liu briefly visited his old master there during the course of 1273, and that was to be the last time the two met. Jiang Wanli, who was by now in his midseventies, left active service at the end of 1273. He moved to Raozhou in Jiangxi, where he arranged for a small pond to be dug near his house. He called it "Pond of Standing Water," to symbolize his rejection of the inflow of Mongolian troops. In this pond, Jiang drowned himself in 1275, after Raozhou was taken by Mongolian forces. His suicide deeply affected Liu, who himself decided to withdraw from active society. When he was invited to take a post in the National Historiography Office later that year, he declined it. Over the course of the next two years, Liu received several further offers of government posts, but he chose instead to travel from place to place, expressing his protest against the Mongol rulers by refusing to serve. His resistance was not so dramatic as Jiang Wanli's or so heroic as Wen Tianxiang's, his fellow Luling man, distant relative, and fellow student at White Egret Academy, but Liu felt himself a kindred spirit to these more famous martyrs of the Mongol resistance.

In the more than twenty years between 1276, when Liu refused to take up the posts offered to him, and his death in 1297, Liu did not pursue active government service. During these years, he had no contact with those involved in statecraft and politics and he shied away from all association with public life. He traveled very little, apart from occasional visits to friends or monasteries and one trip with his son in 1284 to the old Song capital Lin'an, where they mourned the loss of what they regarded as their dynasty.

Interestingly enough, what we do know about Liu Chenweng's life has little to do with the first forty-odd years of it—during which time he achieved examination success, briefly held government posts, and traveled in the entourage of one of the highest-ranking officials of that time—and much more with what he chose to do during these twenty years spent quietly at home in Luling.

Having dedicated over thirty years to the kind of learning that would qualify him for a government position, he now faced a future without an obvious career path. The position he found himself in was not an unusual one. Many men who had spent long years mastering the Confucian classics and preparing for the examinations never got beyond the system's first hurdles. For the majority of the men who had the means to continue their studies to the stage of locally held examinations, the competition was simply too fierce. Not even all of the select few who passed at the highest levels were able to obtain positions in the civil service. The establishment of the alien Mongol regime and the suspension of all examinations after 1274 increased those numbers yet again. Men who had committed themselves to preparation for an official career, which would have provided them with not only justification for their long and arduous existence as students but also with an income, prestige, and social standing, had to look for alternatives. What would their role, and their position, in society be?

A number of important recent studies have shown that, already during the Song dynasty, achieving examination success and holding a post in the civil service were not the only paths to prestige and social standing. Peter Bol has demonstrated how participation alone, as opposed to examination success in the examination culture, could confer standing. His work has also shown that intellectually, participation in the Learning of the Way (*daoxue*) movement justified withdrawal from the examination competition. The *daoxue* movement emphasized the importance of classical learning and moral self-cultivation above learning solely for the purpose of examination success. The gradual acceptance of *daoxue* as state orthodoxy and its increasingly widespread popularity in scholarly circles must have contributed to the choice of many learned men to dedicate themselves to a life of learning, writing, and teaching independent of the examination culture. The fame of such locally based intellectuals, the sheer numbers of extant literary collections, and the complex lineages of teachers and students all testify to the popularity of this choice. Linda Walton's study of Southern Song academies has recently brought to our attention another dimension of intellectual life during the period. Academies, which flourished during the Southern Song, were centers of learning that attracted both local members of the scholarly elite and students from other regions. Although preparation for the examinations was one of the justifications for a stay at an academy, membership in an academy community also offered association and interaction with the social and cultural elite. Academies helped to legitimize and further integrate the cultural and social elites independently of the examinations.

During the Yuan dynasty, when entry into the civil service was severely restricted for members of the Han population in the south, holding a post in an academy was one of the very few available options for examination graduates. Those who could not afford to dedicate themselves to academic, aesthetic, and frivolous pursuits found themselves employed, for example, as medical or religious practitioners, as clerks in local offices, or as tutors of elementary students. Liu Chenweng's choice not to serve the Yuan, but to live in retirement withdrawn from society, was a voluntary one, with which he expressed his loyalty to the old regime. His decision to stay at home to teach and write seems to have been fueled more by feelings of loyalty to and nostalgia for the old status quo and its association with his old mentor than protest against the new and the alien. In fact, toward the end of his life he met with a Mongol leader and wrote a text commemorating their visit. If he did not manifest himself as an anti-Mongol activist, what did he see as his role? He was financially secure enough to enable him to write and teach in his home without having to seek employment elsewhere. His prose writings and letters convey which issues were important to him during this time and how he envisioned his role and position in society. To these writings we now turn.

WRITINGS AND EDUCATION

Despite, or perhaps because of, the changed circumstances after the fall of the Song and the establishment of an alien regime, men like Liu Chenweng continued to devote themselves to the task of preserving the written record of the past for the benefit of future generations. The written record, in their eyes the repository of the values and morals of the past, encompassed various literary genres, poetry among them. A great deal of Liu Chenweng's creative energies were reserved for editing and annotating the poetry of the major Tang poets, including Wang Wei, Du Fu, Meng Haoran, and Li He. He also wrote poetry, and his literary collection contains large numbers of mostly lyrical poems (*ci*). Many of the poems give expression to Liu's sense of sadness over the fall of the Song dynasty. They feature the places, the festivals, and the gatherings of scholars associated with the Southern Song and mourn their loss. Although such poems were, of course, public expressions of his response to the changed political circumstances, they are at the same time very private expressions of Liu's emotional life.

Education is another topic that receives frequent attention in Liu's writings. He was particularly interested in academies; there are more inscriptions for academies attributed to Liu Chenweng than to any other Song writer. He wrote inscriptions for the White Egret Islet Academy in Luling and for two other academies in Jizhou, but also for academies farther afield, such as those in Hunan and Fujian provinces. His inscription for the White Egret Islet Academy is written in part to celebrate the achievements of Liu's mentor, Jiang Wanli, the founder of the academy. But Liu also reflects on what he sees as the ambiguous role of such educational institutions as the White Egret Academy, when he exclaims, "Who can seek his ambitions outside the schools and examinations, but at the same time, who can achieve those ambitions within the schools and examinations?" In other words, he recognized that educational establishments were necessary to initiate a person's learning process but he also argued that fulfilling the ambition that Confucian learning instilled in one could not be achieved solely within that context. They would have to be continually developed within the individual to come to fruition.

Liu, who had started his career as headmaster at an academy, often traveled later in his life to academies, visiting for shorter or longer periods of time. White Egret Islet Academy continued to hold a special place in his heart because of its links with its founder Jiang Wanli. But Liu was not an active member of the *daoxue* fellowship and in his writings he did not promote academies as places that could bring about fundamental change in people and in society. He did not represent them as fundamentally different from prefectural schools; in fact, the close ties between the prefectural school in Luling and White Egret Islet Academy are often remarked upon in inscriptions chronicling the history of these establishments. Both institutions offered opportunities for learning for examinations as well as for self-cultivation. As far as Liu was concerned, they had one more function: they were places where locally influential men could be remembered and venerated. The shrine for White Egret Academy founder Jiang Wanli, established in the late thirteenth century, represented him as a man who had contributed greatly to local culture. For Liu, academies were local institutions that brought local benefits. But he did not believe academies brought about fundamental changes in the way people thought, as some influential *daoxue* thinkers had represented them.

By writing poetry and being involved in teaching and education, Liu Chenweng established himself as a member of the local elite and made a name for himself as a prominent member of the local intelligentsia. His poetry and his involvement in local education both as a teacher and as an active member of White Egret Academy are what Liu Chenweng is known for today. His extant lyrical poetry was collected and edited in a 1998 publication, and his portrait hangs in the recently restored White Egret Academy in Luling, next to his own teacher Ouyang Shoudao and the martyr of the Southern Song, Wen Tianxiang.

There is one other subject of interest that appears prominently in Liu's writings: the temples and shrines of Luling. He wrote extensively on matters pertaining to religion, and this subject will be discussed in greater detail below. It will become clear that writing about temples and monasteries was as important for Liu as, or perhaps even more important than, writing about academies and composing poetry in terms of presenting himself to his peers and his environment as a man of standing and influence on the local scene.

LIU'S TEMPLE INSCRIPTIONS

Apart from writing poetry, editing collections of poetry, and writing for local academies, Liu often wrote commemorative pieces for temples and sacred buildings, sometimes in response to a request from the abbot or from influential members of the temple community. These texts, usually referred to as temple inscriptions, were carved in stone and placed near the entrance to the temple or shrine. Such inscriptions chronicled the history of a temple, mentioned famous visitors and patrons, and frequently made reference to recent restorations or extensions to the buildings. Because the inscriptions were carved in stone and put on display, such texts functioned to signal the importance of this place to its visitors, especially when famous individuals wrote the texts. Among Liu's extant writings there are several dozens of such inscriptions, many of them written for religious establishments located in Jizhou. These texts reveal another aspect of Liu Chenweng's active life.

A number of Liu's temple inscriptions emphasize that there is a close link between the temple and local society. From his texts, we learn that temples were vibrant places at the heart of local activities. Of one temple, he writes, people worship a stone in the shape of a man lying flat. The stone is preserved inside a cave near the River Gan in Jishui County, just north of Luling County. The stone had received continuous worship since the beginning of the Song dynasty in the late tenth century, and at the time of Liu's writing, the deity of this temple embodied by this stone, had recently received an official title. When deities were thought to have brought blessings to the state or to the local people, the central government often recorded the names of the deities and their temples in the official register of beneficent deities, and bestowed honorary titles on such deities. This practice of enfeoffing local deities, which went hand in hand with the rejection and suppression of cults deemed inappropriate, was particularly prevalent during the Southern Song. It offered the representatives of the central government an opportunity to claim some authority over such locally powerful deities, whereby the central state granted a certain prestige and standing to the area's officials and literati, who usually cooperated on such requests for state recognition. In this instance, Liu Chenweng wrote his inscription to celebrate the honorary title that had been bestowed on the deity of this temple.

It is likely, although not made explicit in this example, that the local official who sought central government recognition for this deity also approached Liu Chenweng with a request to mark this recognition in an inscription. His text complies with that request, but Liu does not dwell on the official recognition of this temple. The emphasis Liu chooses in this text conveys a slightly different agenda. It seems that Liu wrote this inscription to convince his audience, which may have included literati and literate clergy and officials from beyond the region, that this temple had a particularly local quality. He does this in several ways. For example, he incorporates a story about the origins of the stone that was worshiped here. Apparently, the river that flowed outside this cave had flooded one year. The swollen river carried a raft, complete with punting pole. The raft deposited this stone by the entrance of the cave, and when the water finally subsided, the flood turned out to have caused little harm to the local residents. Ever since, local people had prayed here, and their requests for timely rain and good harvests had always been answered. The stone had even helped local officials catch thieves and bandits. The stone obviously functioned as a guardian spirit for the local area. By incorporating this story in his inscription, Liu Chenweng validated the story. Even though he does not make explicit whether he himself did pray or would pray at this shrine, he endorses and emphasizes the importance of the stone and its worship by the local area.

In the final lines of the inscription, Liu is more specific about the local quality of this temple. A local deity such as this one, Liu writes, has a benefit similar to those of local doctors and midwives. When an illness strikes or a pregnant woman's labor is imminent, one looks to the locally resident medical specialist to take care of such immediate needs. Similarly, this deity provides care and assistance in cases of specifically local needs. At the same time, Liu suggests, the deity's assistance means that people remain honest, hard-working, and satisfied in their daily endeavors. So Liu sees a greater benefit in recognizing this local worship: an efficacious local deity that can answer local needs also safeguards peace and stability in the locality.

Liu Chenweng's desire to emphasize the importance of worship for local cohesion and identity is also manifest in other inscriptions. For example, Liu wrote an inscription for a temple in Jizhou where three immortals, Lord Fuqiu and his pupils Wang and Guo, were worshiped. During the Southern Song and Yuan dynasties, Lord Fuqiu and his two pupils were better known as the Three Huagai Immortals. They took this name from the mountain in Chongren County in nearby Fu prefecture (Fuzhou), where their worship originated and the center of the cult was located. The cult of the Three Huagai Immortals had spread beyond Chongren County into northern Jizhou and had reached Luling, where this temple was built. Of course, the spread of a regional cult such as the Huagai Immortals did not acknowledge administrative borders or prefectures and counties. For Liu Chenweng, however, the borders do seem to have mattered. He takes great care to explain how the mountain ranges in northern Jizhou were linked to those of southern Fuzhou, and how the Huagai Immortals would have reached Jizhou on their travels, lest the reader think the two locations were too remote to be linked.

He also explained at length how this cult had brought great benefit to the local population: during the outbreaks of unrest at the end of the Southern Song, the distant temple, visible on top of its mountain peak, offered solace to the local population, and when they prayed here for relief in times of hardships caused by droughts or insect plagues, a heavenly lantern appeared in the sky, indicating heaven's responsiveness. Again, Liu recognized the importance of worship at this temple for the proper functioning of the farming community, so utterly dependent always on good harvests, not only during the upheavals of the downfall of the Song dynasty. Liu Chenweng was not alone in writing inscriptions for temples that emphasize their local importance; many of his contemporaries wrote similar inscriptions. Moreover, anthropologists and historians of more recent periods in China have also pointed out the crucial importance of temples and shrines for the structure and organization of local society. We may ask, however, why local literati like Liu Chenweng felt the need to emphasize the importance of the local temples for the local society and its well-being, when that probably was quite obvious to the readers of his inscriptions. For the answer, we need to look more closely at the texts, where it becomes clear that Liu Chenweng did not just describe the local practices at temples, he also commented on them. In fact, at times his descriptions are couched in quite critical language. In an inscription written for Dafan temple in Jizhou, he begins with a description of the location of this temple, less than two miles from the Luling city walls. Long ago, this had been a secluded mountain location, but more recently the paths leading up to the main gates of the temple had been restored and were within easy reach of visitors from the town. The temple's origins dated back four hundred years, but at the beginning of the twelfth century an invasion of Jin soldiers had destroyed most of the buildings. For a long time the temple had lain in ruins, until, toward the end of the thirteenth century, a group of monks and officials had raised the funds for a complete restoration.

Thus far Liu's text follows a common pattern for temple inscriptions. We can probably assume that Liu was approached by the people involved in the Dafan restoration project to write this inscription as a way of commemorating the completion of the restoration work. It is interesting to note, then, that instead of praising the efforts of the people involved and celebrating these recent developments, as one might expect, Liu describes current practice. He tells us that nowadays, at the beginning of the new year, people take trips to popular scenic locations, among them Dafan temple. But instead of coming here to devote themselves to meditation and contemplation in a search for the Way of the

Buddha, people come mostly to admire the view and enjoy the beauty of the buildings. By including the temple in their scenic tour, they hope to benefit from the blessings of the Buddha. The only people, according to Liu, whom come here with less frivolous intentions are the seriously ill and the outcasts of society. They come here sighing and crying, hoping to find some relief from their hardships and stay longer. The lack of sincerity in the intentions of the majority of visitors Liu finds objectionable. These people visit often, but do not dedicate themselves to Buddhist principles. Only the most desperate and excluded members of local society dedicate their lives to obtaining the Buddha truth. All others hope to attain the same in merely fleeting visits.

The text written by Liu would have been carved in stone, and the stone placed by the entry to the temple. There, it would have been an impressive signal that this temple was important enough that a prominent local scholar had written about it. The likelihood is, however, that most visitors would have understood that message even without reading the text. The actual text of the inscription, with its critical message, was probably only understood by local officials and scholars like Liu Chenweng himself.

The inscription for Dafan temple is not the only example of Liu's critical voice. In an inscription written for Wugong temple in Jizhou, Liu directs his criticism at Buddhist doctrinal practice in China. He begins by pointing out that, when Buddhism was first introduced into China from India, it did not find many resonances with Chinese modes of thought. The idea of the pervasiveness of suffering in all aspects of life on earth and the idea of aiming to become completely free of all emotional and personal attachments were entirely unfamiliar to the Chinese. As time went on and Buddhism spread throughout China, the theories, commentaries, and explanations associated with Buddhist doctrine continually increased in number. Over time, Liu suggests, this profusion led to questionable practices among Buddhist scholars in China. Buddhist explications were based on those parts of the texts that were easily compatible with Chinese ways of thinking, while those parts that were more difficult to explain were simply ignored.

Liu then makes a comparison to the Confucian tradition, where the great synthesizer Zhu Xi (1130–1200) was able to grasp the essence of the Six Classics and consolidate the various exegeses and commentaries by establishing the Four Books, thereby enabling students to ignore large parts of the scholarly traditions and still be eligible for bureaucratic selection. But although this worked within the Confucian tradition, Liu feels it caused much damage in the Buddhist tradition. He writes that in recent years this task of providing explanations has become all encompassing. Buddhists establish themselves as official teachers and walk around dressed in monks' clothing. Buddhist masters claim to be able to express the significance of ten thousand characters in just one or two words, ignoring basic Buddhist principles as well as the original texts of the sutras. They disregard basic taboos and requirements for monks, and mislead the lay members of the Buddhist communities.

T. Griffith Foulk, a scholar of Song Buddhism, has pointed out that, at this time, a new way of transmitting Buddhism became popular. So-called discourse records were used in Chan Buddhism, brief records of conversations between teachers and students, which helped spread the Buddhist message during this period. Foulk also notes that during the Song dynasty, the so-called flame histories were used to transmit Buddhist stories and teachings. They, like the discourse records, do not rely on systematic expositions of doctrinal and philosophical issues or on careful annotations and explanations of the sutras. Instead, they convey their message in short, witty statements and in enigmatic expressions, aiming for a more spontaneous, sudden insight into the truth of Buddha's teaching than a gradual text-based understanding. Liu's comments would fit with Griffith Foulk's description of Song practice. Liu is clearly critical of such teachers, who use one character to express ten thousand words, and who thereby reach large numbers of the lay population with their more direct, more accessible methods of teaching.

Again, Liu Chenweng uses an inscription to convey a critical message, and, as in the Dafan temple writing, Liu's message would be understood only by very few visitors to Wugong temple. It is clear, however, that Liu has strong feelings about the current practices he describes and uses this opportunity of writing to convey them. For a final example, we turn to an inscription commemorating the completion of a monks' hall at Chengtian Daoist Monastery on Usi Mountain by using a personal link: he describes how he had traveled there himself and had been impressed by the completion of the building works, so that when he was asked to write an inscription in 1285, he was glad to comply. The inscription also ends with another personal link: the two people who had been involved in the process of restoration were both personal friends and men from his own prefecture. He probably wrote the inscription as a personal favor to these two men. Nevertheless, he uses this inscription to express some critical thoughts. Liu explores the links between the monastery itself and the wider mythical realm where worthies dwell. His description of the scenery invokes jade clouds reaching to the heavens, roaming dragons and phoenixes, immediately suggesting the mythical dimension of the space. The first mortals who arrived here found complete wilderness. They opened up the thicket and established themselves here, perching on rocks and drinking from the streams, using grass for clothing and wood for food, gradually creating a place suitable for worship.

Those days were long gone, of course, and the buildings had become luxurious and comfortable. Visitors began to use the buildings for short stays, looking for instant enlightenment. As in the Dafan inscription, this is the aspect that Liu finds most difficult to accept. While this sacred place had previously harbored people who had suffered hardships in their search for immortality, lately people had benefited from these earlier transformations without having to make any efforts or even concessions to luxury and comfort. Liu compares today's visitors with two famous Daoists from the Period of Division, Wang Xizhi (303–361) and Tao Hongjing (452–536). These two men had roamed the mountains and eked out a living in the wilderness for many years before attaining enlightenment, but people now hope to achieve enlightenment in just one short absence from their comfortable abodes. Liu again uses the request for an inscription, and even the personal link he has to the people involved in the building of a monks' hall, to make a critical observation on the current religious practices associated with the establishment.

But why was Liu so critical? Why did he choose these inscriptions to convey his opinions? The answers to these questions must remain to some extent speculative, as the texts provide no explicit evidence. Exploring the links between the evidence found in the inscriptions and the social, cultural, and political circumstances of the period does, however, yield some plausible explanations. During the Yuan dynasty, many literati like Liu Chenweng became actively concerned over a range of aspects of religious culture. Some very prominent Chinese scholars of the Yuan were closely involved with leaders of the Daoist establishment in southern China, and specifically in Jiangxi province. Confucian scholars and Daoist religious leaders alike were concerned about their Chinese cultural heritage during this period of alien rule. They found ways to cooperate during this period, with the Daoists, who had some degree of access to the Mongol leaders, providing the Confucians an entrée to the Mongol court, and the Confucians lending social standing and prestige to the Daoists through their mutual cooperation. Even if Liu Chenweng did not communicate with high Daoist leaders, his interest in religion is fitting in a context where religious practices had become a major subject of interest for literati.

Of course, not all literati concern for religion generally and Daoism specifically revolved around political access and influence. Robert P. Hymes, a scholar of Southern Song and Yuan dynasty religion, suggests in *Statesmen and Gentlemen* that literati were particularly interested in local cults during the Yuan dynasty, because such cults offered worshipers direct means of communication with the objects of worship, as opposed to the more bureaucratic, indirect religious practices associated with Daoism, where little could be achieved without the help of a religious professional. These more direct means of communication with the divine world were congruent, according to Hymes, with the direct, localized ways in which Yuan literati interacted with their surroundings.

Probably, these considerations also held for Liu Chenweng. His interest in local religion might be partly explained by the fact that many of the traditional avenues of interacting with one's environment, particularly by accepting an official position, were closed during his lifetime. That barrier and his critical concern for the religious practices may have been linked to or enhanced by the fact that the inscriptions he contributed offered him a public way of expressing his views in an attempt to bring about change in his local environment.

Liu Chenweng continued to write until mere days before his death in 1297. His literary writing and his students obviously occupied a great deal of his attention during the last twenty years of his life, which he spent away from all official obligations and engagements. But his life during these quiet years was punctuated by regular visits to places of worship and sacred sites. He traveled several times to Mount Lu in the north of Jiangxi province, and visited the numerous temples, shrines, and monasteries hidden in the stunning mountain scenery. He visited the temples in and near the old Song capital at Hangzhou on more than one occasion. But most of his trips were closer to home: he visited temples in almost every Jizhou county, and just across the Jizhou borders in Fuzhou prefecture to the east and Hunan province to the west. He marked many of these visits with an inscription, and there was clearly a strong personal dimension to his visits to these temples.

In the same way that his poetry was not merely a private expression of personal feelings, and his texts for academies reflect more than his private interest in academic affairs, his temple inscriptions were also public statements of his opinions. From his critical tone, we can deduce that he hoped to affect his readers' behavior. In that sense, his temple inscriptions provide us with an insight into the ways in which Liu Chenweng tried to be a "somebody." He had chosen not to be actively involved in politics after the fall of the Yuan, and he had also elected not to become involved in the *daoxue* movement or to be associated with other philosophical groups. He had not, however, completely turned his back on society. His commitment to local society and his active involvement with local practices are manifest in the expression of his views in his temple inscriptions.

The inscriptions, however, reveal little about Liu's own spiritual life. We do not know where he might have prayed, what ceremonies and festivals he might have attended, or what rituals were carried out after his death. It is clear, nevertheless, that religion mattered to Liu Chenweng. When we take stock of his life more than seven hundred years after his death, it is important that we remember not just his poetry and his involvement in White Egret Academy and the other academies he visited, but also his involvement in local religious culture. For Liu Chenweng, writing about religion was one of the ways in which he wished to make his mark in his social and cultural milieu.

SUGGESTED READINGS

Bol, Peter K. *This Culture of Ours: Intellectual Transitions in T'ang and Sung China*. Stanford, 1992.

Ebrey, Patricia Buckley, and Peter N. Gregory, eds. *Religion and Society in T'ang and Sung China*. Honolulu, 1993.

Gregory, Peter N., and Daniel A. Gerz, Jr. *Buddhist in the Sung*. Honolulu, 1999.

Hansen, Valerie. *Changing Gods in Medieval China, 1127-1276*. Princeton, 1990.

Hymes, Robert P. *Statesmen and Gentlemen: The Elite of Fu-chou, Chiang-hsi, in Northern and Southern Sung*. Cambridge, 1986.

Langlois, John D., Jr. *China under Mongol Rule*. Princeton, 1981.

Walton, Linda. *Academies and Society in Southern Sung China*. Honolulu, 1999.

CHAPTER 8

Fang Xiaoru

Moralistic Politics in the Early Ming

PETER DITMANSON

With the expulsion of the Mongols and the establishment of the Ming dynasty the shidafu *(educated, literate elite) once again found themselves the ruling class in the Chinese Empire. But their position was far from unchallenged, nor did its members form a monolithic group in terms of their political thought and practice. The first few decades of the Ming were filled with tension between the founding emperor, Zhu Yuanzhang, and his leading literati officials. Zhu repeatedly purged high-ranking leaders and carried out bloody inquisitions against any who he thought opposed his rule. After his death in 1398, his grandson, more sympathetic to the interests of the* shi *and the proprieties of Confucianism, came to the throne, but he was overthrown just four years later by his uncle Zhu Di, the Prince of Yan. Zhu Di's usurpation of the throne in 1402 presented Confucian officials with a harsh choice: to remain loyal to the deposed emperor and risk their own lives, or accept service under the new ruler and compromise their principles and ideals.*

Fang Xiaoru chose the former course and became a martyr to his Confucian values. Peter Ditmanson, assistant professor of history at Colby College, presents Fang in the context of literati politics and imperial power in the early Ming. The literati were meant to embody the moral order, and in men such as Fang they did so. They continued to occupy the center stage of Ming society. But, as we will see in subsequent chapters, the shi *had to contend not only with the awesome power of emperors but also with other centers of power and prestige in a rapidly changing China.*

In the summer of 1402, Fang Xiaoru stood before the new ruler of the Ming dynasty. Zhu Di had just wrested the throne from his twenty-five-year-old nephew, Zhu Yunwen, in a bloody three-year civil war that culminated with the imperial palace at Nanjing in ashes. The body of Zhu Yunwen, grandson of the founder of the dynasty, was never found. He had probably perished in the palace fire, though rumors persisted that he might have escaped by wandering about the empire disguised as a Buddhist monk.

Fang Xiaoru had been one of the highest-ranking advisers to the dead emperor, and he was now summoned before the new emperor and ordered to prepare a declaration of the new reign, entitled "Yongle" (Eternal Joy). The new emperor knew that Fang, as a prominent servant of the preceding reign, would lend further credibility to the declaration. He explained to Fang that he had intervened in the affairs of the court because his young nephew had been ill advised by other family members and by unscrupulous counselors. He likened the situation to that of the noble Duke of Zhou in high antiquity who guarded his young nephew, King Cheng, from the evil machinations of his uncles and other predators.

Fang Xiaoru was unmoved, and asked, "Then, where is King Cheng?" The exasperated Zhu Di refused to discuss his dead nephew further and ordered Fang's execution. In keeping with the traditional view that one's relations shared in one's guilt, the Emperor further ordered the liquidation of all of Fang's family members and associates, more than eight hundred people, by some estimates.

Fang's death at the age of forty-five brought an end to the brilliant career of one of the most talented and influential statesmen and thinkers of the early Ming period. The dramatic fluctuations in his career are worth our examination, for they shed light upon the broader social and political circumstances of this tumultuous era in Chinese history. Some of the details of his life are sketchy, for all materials written by him or about him were strictly banned. Anyone found in possession of writings by Fang Xiaoru was executed. It was not until the later decades of the fifteenth century that his biography and a collection of his writings were pieced together.

Fang was born in 1357, in the waning years of the Mongol Yuan dynasty (1271–1368). By this time, the empire was in shambles. Famines and floods on the Yellow River had brought great social and economic upheaval, exacerbated by administrative factionalism, ineptitude, and corruption. Rebellions broke out in several parts of China, some in the form of millenarian religious groups. From one of these groups in the south, the Red Turbans, emerged Zhu Yuanzhang, a peasant who rose to become a regional strongman around the Nanjing area. Zhu went on to found the new Ming dynasty (1368–1644) among the ruins of the Yuan, and he titled his reign Hongwu, "Martial Grandeur."

Fang came from a prominent family in the area of Ninghai on the northern coast of Zhejiang, a region that came under Zhu Yuanzhang's rule in the 1360s. At that time, the Fangs were not famous throughout the empire, but they were well known in their locality. Fang took great pride in his family heritage and enumerated their achievements in the funerary biography that he wrote for his father. For generations, he explained, his family had revered scholarly pursuits and had served as ritual specialists for the community. His great-grandfather had passed the civil service examinations at the local level and had become a teacher of some renown. His great-grandmother was a descendant of a Song dynasty prime minister. His grandfather had served as a regional director of schools.

Fang's father, Fang Keqin (1326–76) was a man of considerable talent and ambition. The younger Fang's biography of his father describes his education as a young man*:

> From his birth, my father was dignified and unusual. When he was five, he could read books and parse the passages for himself. When he was ten, he had memorized the Five Confucian Classics. His literary compositions used precocious wording. And the old men of the community would cluck in delight at his novelty, and called him a child genius.
>
> When he was a little older, he read the works of Guan and Min (Zhang Zai, 1020–77, and Zhu Xi, 1140–1200), and sighing, he declared, "Learning should be like this!" He thereby put aside frivolous and flowery composition and set his mind to understanding the complexities of human nature and principles. He closed his doors and discussed and practiced, oblivious to hunger, thirst, cold or heat. By the time he was nineteen, he had thoroughly developed his virtue to become a famous scholar.

By Fang's accounting, then, his father underwent a major transformation in his learning. Moreover, he explained (perhaps with some embellishment), his father led the way to a change in the whole region, leading the people to set aside superficial literary pursuits and engage in serious study. This "conversion" experience of his father and his community, however romanticized in Fang's recounting, had an important shaping role in the direction of Fang's own thought and career. What was this transformation?

Fang here was referring to a collection of teachings and a social movement called *daoxue*, or the "Learning of the Way." This school had developed over the course of the Song dynasty (960–1279), and became structured and formalized by the scholar Zhu Xi. *Daoxue* adherents advocated a highly moralistic program of self-cultivation based upon the curriculum of Confucian texts laid out by Zhu Xi and his peers. They had criticized the learning practices fostered by the civil service examination system, which called for broad encyclopedic learning and rote memorization. And they eschewed literary efforts, the composition of lofty poetry or ornate prose, which they regarded as supercilious and amoral.

---

*All quotes from Fang's writings are from Fan Xiaoru, *Xunzhizhai* (Ningbo, 1996).

Over the thirteenth and fourteenth centuries, bitter partisan battles had raged between the *daoxue* adherents and their opponents who considered them narrow and pretentious. In 1313, a few years before Fang's father was born, the *daoxue* advocates had won over the court of the Mongol Yuan. Their progenitors were honored at the Confucian temple at the capital, and their teachings were made the official curriculum of the civil service exams. Thus the transformation that Fang Xiaoru described in his father's biography marked a shift away from the family's older scholarly traditions to an adoption of the now politically dominant *daoxue* school.

Despite his commitment to these teachings, his father Fang Keqin failed the 1344 civil service examinations. The son blamed this failure upon official corruption among the examiners. Fang Keqin was thus barred from service under the ailing Yuan dynasty. During these years, however, he maintained his stature as a scholar, traveling around to study and teach on his own.

We do not know very much about Fang Xiaoru's mother, Madame Lin. She died in 1364, and although Fang was only five years old, people said that he mourned her with all the propriety of an adult. Fang wrote very little about her. He mentioned her in his biography of his father, noting her natal family, and praising her "wifely virtue that surpassed all other generations of the clan." Such terse treatment of women's biographies was not unusual. Scholars like Fang wrote occasionally about women of exemplary moral virtue, but in general, women were not prominently recognized in *daoxue* circles, which emphasized the transmission of learning from male masters to male disciples.

The Fang family fortunes changed quite rapidly with the foundation of the new Ming dynasty under Zhu Yuanzhang in 1368. Three years later, when Fang's father was forty-five years old, he passed a civil service examination offered at the capital. He was then assigned as a prefect in southern Shandong. Here and in his successive posts, the elder Fang developed a reputation as an able, just, and benevolent administrator. In his jurisdiction, he deterred gangs of marauding bandits (prevalent in the early Ming), built schools, and alleviated the heavy tax burdens on the populace.

Along with the honors of increasing recognition and renown, however, came growing risks inherent in the world of civil service in the early years of the dynasty. The Hongwu emperor, a former peasant, bore a deep distrust of the officials of the realm and chastised them in fearsome and unpredictable ways. In 1376, Fang's father fell victim when his name appeared on a list of officials whose bureaucratic practices the emperor found improper. In fact, these officials had followed a standard if unofficial shortcut, presigning blank forms to expedite shipments of tax revenue from their localities up to the capital. The emperor regarded these procedures as bureaucratic malfeasance, and ordered the execution of all those involved. At great personal risk, the younger Fang petitioned the court to allow him to serve a prison term on his father's behalf, but he was ignored. Shortly afterward, his father died in prison.

Fang was twenty-nine when his father died in 1376. He followed the proper procedures for burying and mourning his father, and, as required by ritual protocol, he made no career moves for three years. He did, however, continue to pursue his own studies and to develop important connections in academic and political circles.

The year his father died, Fang traveled to the nearby prefecture of Jinhua and sought out the tutelage of Song Lian (1310–81), one of the most important men of letters in the empire. For nearly two decades, Song had served as a personal adviser to the emperor and tutor to the heir apparent, while holding a series of high-ranking civil posts at court. He had directed several large projects on the emperor's behalf, including the compilation of a history of the preceding dynasty, an account of the Ming imperial conquest, a compendium of ritual prescriptions, and an imperial calendar. His own literary writings were highly regarded and were sought out by scholars from as far away as Korea and Japan. That Fang Xiaoru sought him out as a teacher was a measure of the young man's scholarly and political ambitions.

The year after Fang joined him, Song Lian retired, and returned to his native Jinhua, in central Zhejiang, some 200 kilometers west of Fang's Ninghai home. Jinhua was renowned for a long and established tradition of learning. Since the twelfth century, this place had fostered numerous prominent men of letters. Some were from this area; others had come here to teach. With great pride, Song Lian and others often referred to Jinhua as "the land of literature."

Jinhua was known for its rich scholastic traditions as well. Numerous important thinkers and teachers were identified with this place. Most notably, the people here laid claim to a lineage of *daoxue* teachers who traced their intellectual pedigree back to the scholar Zhu Xi himself. Hence, Jinhua natives argued that theirs was an authoritative transmission and that learning about *daoxue* from them was virtually like learning it from Zhu Xi.

Fang Xiaoru found these claims persuasive and came to Jinhua to participate in the great traditions of this scholastic center. He revered Song Lian and took great pride in becoming his student. In Song he found the moral authority of Jinhua's *daoxue* teachings combined with the talent and refinement of Jinhua's literary traditions. The sentiment was mutual, for Song Lian was deeply impressed by Fang's talents as a writer and as a thinker.

Fang greatly admired his own father, but by Fang's account of him, he was largely self-taught, and did not seem to have had significant training under a known master. It is perhaps for this reason that throughout the rest of his life, Fang traced his own intellectual lineage back through Jinhua rather than through his own family. He frequently wrote admiring pieces about Jinhua. For example, in an epitaph for a man named Zheng from that area, he praised its rich heritage: "My generation of lesser men unfortunately did not have the chance to see Jinhua in its heyday. Those we have been able to see number five or six, including Song Lian and [a list of prominent local scholars]. These men were the elite of a hundred generations. And Master Zheng emerged in their midst, with exchanges back and forth with necks outstretched, debating up and down, like bright stars in a constellation, like gold and precious stones reflecting off of each other."

Fang's studies in Jinhua linked him to this "constellation" and brought him great prestige. As the prize pupil of Song Lian, he soon became the primary heir to the rich traditions of Jinhua and, eventually, its most prominent spokesman.

Beyond its scholarly preeminence, Jinhua held an important political role in Fang's thinking as well. Fang had a deep antipathy toward the Mongol Yuan dynasty that had preceded the Ming; he regarded the Mongols as barbarians and those who served them as misguided. In a piece he composed for a friend, Fang described his view of the effects of Mongol rule on his hometown: "Then came the Yuan, which seduced the realm into the pursuit of profit. The masses flocked to this, and their scholastic habits became empty pretense. Those with skill and nerve got ahead through unrestrained bullying. Those fond of wealth and extravagance found gratification in arrogant idleness. And the old customs of the Song [the dynasty that preceded the Yuan] grew dim."

In Fang's view, the legitimate source of cultural authority during those dark years of the Yuan lay in Jinhua, and not at the Mongol capital at Dadu (Beijing). In the same epitaph for Master Zheng, cited above, he reiterated this point: "The people cannot live on their own. There must be a ruler to look over them. But the precariousness of Our Way is such that it cannot be without corruption. If there are no worthies, then no one can raise it from decline and keep it from falling. Therefore, in the nearly 100 years since the fall of the Song, the people have looked towards Jinhua, with its brilliant transmission."

Hence for Fang, the culture and scholarship of Jinhua was the crucial link between his own dynasty and the legacy of Chinese civilization itself. The legitimacy of the Ming lay not in its succession from the Yuan, but in its inheritance of the culture and scholarship of Jinhua and men such as Song Lian.

In 1360, when Zhu Yuanzhang was still just a regional warlord, he handpicked Song to serve as tutor to his five-year-old son, Zhu Biao, the heir apparent. Although not much is known about the particulars of this relationship, it is clear that the heir apparent had great respect for Song Lian and the traditions of learning that he represented. In the early years of the dynasty, the founding emperor had relied heavily upon Jinhua scholars. He recognized *daoxue* teachings as authoritative, and endorsed them insofar as they did not challenge his own authority.

But over the course of his reign, the Hongwu emperor grew increasingly suspicious and impatient with the bureaucratic apparatus of the empire, ordering countless executions and numerous purges. In 1380, the emperor launched a massive purge of officials who were connected to the prime minister, whom he suspected of treason. One of those implicated was a grandson of Fang's teacher Song Lian. The grandson was ordered executed, and Song Lian himself was spared only by the intervention of the empress and the heir apparent. Instead of execution, he was sent to distant exile in the northwest corner of Sichuan province. Old and enfeebled, he died en route, under the rigors of the journey.

Fang was devastated by the death of Song Lian. In subsequent years, he worked hard to have his mentor's writings published. He wrote several prayers to the spirit of Song Lian, in which he praised the teacher's great contributions to the empire and vowed to sustain his legacy. Song Lian once appeared to him in a dream, saying, "I must transmit Our Culture. If not to you, then to whom?" Fang's dream was largely borne out, for after the passing of Song Lian, he was broadly recognized as the heir of the traditions of Jinhua.

No doubt with some trepidation, Fang journeyed to the capital in 1383 to offer his services to the Hongwu emperor whose rages had brought on the deaths of his father and his teacher. No appointment came from the interview, and Fang was sent home to Ninghai, where he taught and wrote. He made a second visit to the capital in 1392. This time, the emperor received him cordially, acknowledging his scholarship and fame. He declined, however, to give Fang a significant appointment, assigning him instead to serve as an education director in the distant prefecture of Hanzhong in southwestern Shanxi. The journey to his post with his family took over three months.

Although this remote appointment and difficult teaching conditions there were clearly disappointing, Fang nevertheless maintained his correspondence with colleagues and remained one of the most influential scholars in the empire. In fact, shortly after his arrival in Hanzhong in the spring of 1393, he was summoned back to administer the provincial civil service examinations for the metropolitan district around the capital at Nanjing. This was a prestigious post that acknowledged his scholarly preeminence and his relationship to Song Lian, who had conducted those examinations more than twenty years earlier.

At the conclusion of the examinations, Fang wrote a commemorative inscription for the event. As was customary for one in his position, Fang praised the inspirational role of the court in the bountiful yield of a new crop of virtuous and educated civil servants. The court, he held, had restored education in the empire from the depths that it had reached under the Mongols. "And why is it that so many scholars are compelled to study? It is truly that His Highness's mind is full of wise plans for governance rectified with Heaven, and that Heaven has responded to this. Heaven desires to spread bounty throughout the empire, and therefore silently aids Him, bestowing men of worthy talent to Him. These myriad worthies assemble at court, and the numerous men of talent are arrayed at their posts."

Fang himself had not taken the civil service examinations. One of the reasons for this was that the Hongwu emperor had been disappointed in this route of official recruitment and had canceled them in 1373. They were not reinstated until 1384. As a *daoxue* advocate, Fang had reservations of his own about the examinations as an effective gauge of moral caliber and administrative potential. In his 1393 commemoration, he had also addressed these concerns.

> It is said the court chooses scholars through their literary composition [in the exams]. But the expectations of these scholars are not simply literary. As scholars rise through the examinations, for the fulfillment of their person they cannot rely upon the examinations. They must all step beyond this and advance further. For that which the noble man studies is the way of the sages. And in the way of the sages, there is nothing more important than benevolence, righteousness, integrity and filial piety. A scholar must hold on to benevolence, righteousness, integrity and filial piety, just as a farmer continues to plow, never abandoning it for a day.

Thus, in moralistic tones that were the *daoxue* trademark, Fang here reasserted the need for values and ideals that lay beyond the examinations. This view must have found favor with the court, for in 1396, he was summoned from Hanzhong again to oversee the provincial examinations of the capital metropolitan district.

Through his connections with Song Lian and with the Jinhua region, Fang's authority was recognized by members of the imperial family. Shortly after his assignment to Hanzhong, Fang was eagerly sought out by Prince Xian, (1371–1423), the eleventh son of the founder. The prince had been granted a fief that was centered in the relatively remote city of Chengdu. Like several other members of the imperial family, the prince had become acquainted with Jinhua colleagues during his younger years at the capital. Thus he knew of Fang's reputation and seized upon the opportunity to establish a relationship when Fang was assigned to Hanzhong, some 400 kilometers north of the prince's fief.

Fang went to pay his respects to Prince Xian at Chengdu in 1394, and was made tutor to the prince's son, an honorary title, as the boy was not yet five years old. According to records, Fang was treated well by the prince "who forgot protocol and was deferential in his discussions." On this visit, Prince Xian recognized Fang's *daoxue* authority by granting him the title of "Master of Correct Learning." Many of Fang's students and colleagues came to address him by this title. In the years that followed, Fang made frequent visits to the prince, and the two sustained a correspondence that included discussions of literature, philosophy, and personnel matters. Under Fang's urging, the prince provided support to Song Lian's surviving family members and brought some of Fang's Jinhua colleagues into his retinue.

By 1397, Fang and his colleagues had determined that his reputation warranted the publication of his collected writings, an uncommon undertaking for someone of his years. We do not know which of his writings that survive today were included in this original publication. Prefaces to this work do survive, however, and these reaffirm his literary credentials as well as his *daoxue* authority. A preface written by his friend and fellow townsman Lin You decried the prevalence of shallow scholarship, tainted with Buddhist and Daoist influences. As for Fang, wrote Lin, "The words he speaks and the theories he holds are all based upon highest principles and harmonize with Heaven's way, such as have not been seen since the time of the Cheng brothers and Zhu Xi (Song dynasty founders of *daoxue*). Of the dedicated scholars of the realm, there are none who can best his words and theories, and they all abandon their own learning to follow him." Here and in the other prefaces, Fang was acknowledged as a leading man of letters, and as a champion of *daoxue* learning.

Fang wrote extensively about *daoxue*. The literature of this school tended toward technical jargon and arcane philosophical debate, but Fang preferred to write homiletic pieces for ordinary people. He frequently wrote simple poems with specific advice. His writings included, for example, a set of inscriptions for different objects in the home. One was written for a bookshelf:

> Ah, the way of the many sages,
> is all collected right here.
> If you cannot reflect deeply and study hard,
> then these books will be empty tools.
> If you cannot emulate the worthies and follow the sages,
> then your learning will not be true knowledge.
> The petty man, the supreme fool,

dares to not be reverent and cautious.
Each day, remain diligent.

Another was composed for a bedroom pillow:

Upon this spot, reflect upon the Way,
and the Way will become clear.
On this spot, discuss problems,
and the problems will be resolved.
On this spot, be vigilant,
and your prosperity will magnify.
On this spot, be licentious,
and disasters will arrive.

Like most *daoxue* fundamentalists, Fang believed that such attention to rigorous moral detail in one's own life was the bedrock of self-cultivation and enlightenment.

Fang frequently voiced contempt for the state of scholarship in his day. In a piece he wrote on methods of learning, he described his concerns: "I have doubts about today's 'scholars of the Classics.' As children, they chant them. Then they pirate the empty words to obtain profit and reward. This is like bringing home a tub of food to feed the family, and then abandoning them without regard. If you ask them what this is called, they say 'comprehending the Classics.' But if you ask them about the way of the Classics, they say, 'I do not know!' "

He railed further against those who refused to base their statecraft upon the Confucian Classics: "If you ask them why they do this, they say, 'The Classics are of insufficient use!' Alas! Can this be called learning the Classics? If a Classic is without use, how can it be a Classic? But this is not the fault of the Classics. It is the stupidity of those who study them. And it is not even the stupidity of those who study, it is the lack of methods of those who teach them."

Throughout such essays, Fang argued for the need for comprehensive study of the Classics. And a true understanding of these, he asserted, came through the guidance of the masters of the *daoxue* school. Fang was also aware, however, that there were many in the realm who found fault with the moralistic stance of *daoxue* advocates. In a practice examination question, he ordered his students to wrestle with this problem: "In recent generations, there have been numerous great Confucians who have assertively called themselves *daoxue*. The ordinary people of our times, however, have disparaged them and not believed in them. Some have attacked them for being a faction. Some have regarded them as fakes. Why is this?"

It was clear that Fang wanted his students to answer these critics with a defense of his school, but he nonetheless conceded the partisanship that *daoxue* and its enemies had engendered.

Just before Fang was sent to remote Hanzhong, the Ming court suffered a crisis that destabilized the empire for the next decade. In the spring of 1392, Zhu Biao, the heir apparent, died of illness, leaving the court bereft of a successor to the aging Hongwu emperor. After five months of intense deliberation, the founder appointed Zhu Biao's son, the fifteen-year-old Zhu Yunwen, to be the next emperor, in keeping with his policy of primogeniture. This assignment was good news for *daoxue* advocates such as Fang, for this branch of the imperial family had been close to the scholars of Jinhua since the early days when the child Zhu Biao had been tutored by Song Lian.

The appointment of Hongwu's grandson was disappointing, however, to some of his other sons who felt that they should have been chosen. Prominent among these was Zhu Di, who was known for his military prowess and had played an important role in managing the imperial garrisons to the north that protected the empire from Mongol raids. His fief in the north was thus well fortified with a large army at his disposal. Hence, Zhu Di and some of the other uncles of the young heir apparent felt far more qualified to continue the strong military legacy established by their founding father.

In the summer of 1398, the Hongwu emperor died and his grandson came to the throne with the decidedly unmartial reign title of "Jianwen," (Establishing Culture). Upon the suggestion of his advisers, the young emperor soon summoned Fang Xiaoru to serve in the Hanlin Academy, the prestigious scholarly establishment that provided advice to the throne and drafted imperial edicts and other court documents. Fang continued to rise through the echelons of the court. In 1399, he was granted the rare honor of presiding for a third time over the provincial exams of the capital district. In 1400, he directed the highest level of exams in Nanjing for an empirewide slate of candidates. By the conventions of Chinese literati culture, the 110 students who passed the exam that year were obliged to Fang with a lasting student–teacher bond of loyalty. Although there remained others at court who outranked him, this appointment established Fang as the highest scholarly authority in the realm.

Later that year, Fang was made editor in chief of a large encyclopedia project commissioned by the new emperor. These editors would collect documents culled from the entire corpus of the Chinese literary tradition, and the compilation would be used for pedagogical and hortatory purposes. Under Fang's direction was a group of the best scholars of the realm, including some who had placed at the top of the most recent civil service examination.

Over the course of this ill-fated reign, Fang gradually emerged as one of the young emperor's most trusted advisers. Fang had strong views on governance and the ways of moral leadership, and he made these views known. Like other *daoxue* proponents, Fang believed in the restoration of the idealized order of high antiquity, as outlined in the Confucian Classics. Some of his critics argued that he took these views to impractical extremes. He believed, for example, that the land ownership in rural areas should be restructured into the communal pattern described in the *Rites of Zhou*.*

Among Fang's concerns was the definition of moral rulership. He conceded broad power and authority to the throne, but he argued that this power came with formidable moral obligations. These obligations necessitated careful attendance by the emperor to the words of his advisers. Fang's outspoken views circumscribing imperial power would not have found a sympathetic ear at the court of the autocratic Hongwu emperor, but they seem to have gained credence at his grandson's throne.

Like many thinkers before him, Fang believed that the great sage–kings of China's antiquity had been chosen by Heaven to bring order and civility to the passionate savagery of primitive humans. To illustrate this distinction in status, the ruler was blessed with material possessions that would empower him to lead. "So his residence was enlarged and his carriages were made splendid, and he was given the greatest of the jewels and curios between Heaven and earth. This was to fix his heart upon the affairs of the people. Therefore, Heaven established the ruler on behalf of the people, rather than giving the people to the ruler."

Such wealth then was an implement in the ruler's dispensation of his duties, as well as a rewarding incentive for sustaining his vigil. The problems emerged, explained Fang, when the common people became bedazzled by this wealth, and began to confer greater and greater powers upon the ruler. And they became increasingly dependent upon him to assuage all of their sufferings. Thus, the relationship between ruler and subject became distorted, with the common people worshiping the ruler and plying him with offerings.

Corrupt rulers, argued Fang, took advantage of this confusion: "The rulers in later generations understood that the responsibilities of the people were to serve their superior, but they did not understand that the responsibility of the ruler was to nurture the people."

---

*This pattern, called the well-field system, involved squares divided into nine sections (like a tic-tac-toe game), with the middle square as a public center with a well and other communal resources.

Hence, it was not only confusion among the populace, but negligence on the part of China's rulers, that had led to the decline from the ideal order of high antiquity.

What, then, was the solution? For Fang, it lay in the proper education of the ruler. And in his writings, he outlined his views on this as well. The ruler, argued Fang, cultivates his mind above all else. This had been a stock admonition among *daoxue* advocates at court, but Fang articulated this position in a more forthright manner than his predecessors had. In his view, the ruler ought to put the cultivation of his mind above all else. The ancient sages, he argued, "all took the rectification of the mind as their basis. If the ruler rectifies the mind in regard to all under Heaven, then the wise will plan for him; the benevolent will protect him; the brave will fight for him; and those scholars with talent will all exert themselves in the application of their skills." Hence, for Fang, the role of the emperor was that of a moral beacon, with the administration of the empire left in the hands of his subordinates, men like Fang himself.

It appears that the young Jianwen emperor valued the counsel of Fang and others and took an interest in the policies they proposed. Historians can only speculate, however, on the larger vision of the Jianwen emperor, for his realm was soon destabilized by political turmoil that erupted into civil war in 1399, the second year of his reign. One of the root causes was the designs of the young ruler's uncles and his efforts to curb their ambitions. The war ended when Zhu Di's northern armies entered Nanjing, and fires destroyed the imperial palace.

Few reliable accounts of the Jianwen reign survive, and little is known of the actual policies and programs that were implemented. The documents and records of this period were largely altered or destroyed after the usurpation of the throne. This four-year reign was obliterated from the histories, and those years were simply included in the founder's reign.

The new Yongle emperor had sought to draw upon Fang's unassailable political and scholarly credentials to bring legitimacy to his reign. In accordance with his fundamentalist *daoxue* views of moral rulership, Fang would not comply. Thereupon, by executing Fang and his family and colleagues and banning his writings, Yongle intended to eclipse his place in history.

In the long run, the emperor did not succeed. Yongle himself later acknowledged that Fang had indeed been a loyal servant of his sovereign (one of the highest ideals in Chinese civil service). His son and successor, the Hongxi emperor (1425–26), also extolled the virtues of Fang and the other martyrs of the usurpation and restored some of the confiscated lands of their clans.

In spite of the official bans, Fang's legacy persisted, and by the 1460s, an edition of his writings was published cautiously. By the end of the century, biographies were compiled that reconstructed some of the events of Fang's life. Scholars also wrote praises of his wife and children, who reportedly preceded him in death through honorable suicide in 1402.

Over the course of the sixteenth century, numerous scholars called for the vindication of Fang's life and career, until a comprehensive pardon was issued for all the descendants of the martyrs of the 1402 usurpation. Many in this period looked back on the early Ming with idealized nostalgia for a time that they regarded as more upright than their own. To them, Fang was revered as a model of integrity.

After the fall of the Ming dynasty in 1644, Fang's ideas about rulership and statecraft found currency among men like Huang Zongxi (1610–95) and other political theorists of the early Qing dynasty (1644–1912). These ideas, centering around the obligations of the ruler to his people, were eventually drawn into service by the early republican Chinese thinkers at the turn of the twentieth century.

But what of Fang's immediate legacy in the early Ming period? After the execution of the top echelons of his predecessor's court, the Yongle emperor recruited a new coterie of scholars and advisers to rebuild the cultural authority of the throne. Several of these new men had passed the examinations in 1400 under Fang's direction. And, like Fang, all of them had reputations as men of considerable literary talent, talent derived from local traditions throughout the empire. But most of these men had little or no apparent interest in *daoxue* and no connections to Jinhua or the other centers of *daoxue* scholarship. Some of them were critics of the adherents of *daoxue*, not unlike those that Fang had described.

Like his brothers, the Yongle emperor had probably been steeped in *daoxue* teachings at the hands of Fang's Jinhua colleagues. While he acknowledged the authority of *daoxue* teachings, however, he claimed the mantle of that authority for himself, rather than yielding it to the masters in Jinhua or elsewhere. And throughout the course of his reign, he presided over the reconstruction of *daoxue* as a court-centered tradition, with imperially sponsored schools and an imperially commissioned curriculum of authoritative texts.

Fang's school of *daoxue* learning had emerged victorious as the undisputed wisdom of the empire. In the service of an autocratic ruler, however, and in the hands of ambivalent men with no connections to the earlier traditions of the school, *daoxue* had lost its partisan edge and its moralist platform. The era of Fang Xiaoru had ended.

SUGGESTED READINGS

Chan, David B. *The Usurpation of the Prince of Yen, 1398–1402*. San Francisco, 1976.

Chan Hok-lam. "The Chien-wen, Yung-lo, Hung-hsi and Hsuan-te Reigns," *Cambridge History of China*, vol. 7:1. Edited by Frederick Mote and Denis Twitchett, 193–202. Cambridge, England, 1988.

Crawford, Robert B., Harry M. Lamley, and Albert B. Mann. "Fang Hsiao-ju in the Light of Early Ming Society." *Monumenta Serica* 15:2 (1956): 303–27.

Dardess, John W. *Confucianism and Autocracy: Professional Elites in the Founding of the Ming Dynasty*. Berkeley, 1983.

Dreyer, Edward L. *Early Ming China : A Political History, 1355–1435*. Stanford, 1982.

Elman, Benjamin. "Where Is King Ch'eng?" *T'oung Pao* 79, no. 3 (1993): 23–68.

Fincher, John. "China as a Race, Culture, and Nation: Notes on Fang Hsiao-ru's Discussion of Dynastic Legitimacy." In *Transition and Permanence: Chinese History and Culture: A Festschrift in Honor of Dr. Hsiao Kung-ch'uan*. Edited by David C. Buxbaum and Frederick W. Mote, 59–69. Hong Kong, 1972.

Langlois, John D., Jr. "The Hung-wu Reign." In *Cambridge History of China*, vol. 7:1. Edited by Frederick Mote and Denis Twitchett, 107–81. Cambridge, England, 1988.

Mote, Frederick. "Fang Hsiao-ju." In *Dictionary of Ming Biography, 1368–1644*. Edited by L. Carrington Goodrich and Chaoying Fang, 426–33. New York, 1976.

CHAPTER 9

The Eunuch Wang Zhen and the Ming Dynasty

KENNETH J. HAMMOND

As the Ming dynasty assumed its fully developed form, the literati found themselves presiding over a society that was increasingly complex and dynamic. The imperial state had to govern a vast territory with a rapidly increasing population and a growing economy. The regular bureaucratic administration, based on the Confucian examination system as its main means of recruiting men for government service, came to be supplemented by a wide variety of quasi-official or subofficial roles that augmented the functions of regular offices. In addition, Ming emperors came to rely heavily on eunuchs, castrated males in personal service to the throne, to carry out administrative tasks.

Wang Zhen, whose life is recounted in this chapter, takes us into the realm of the eunuchs in the imperial palace and how they came to exercise great power from the middle years of the fifteenth century onward. The role played by these imperial agents created a counterbalance to the dominance of the literati and gave the monarchy a means to control, and sometimes to intimidate, the Confucian scholars–officials. Eunuchs in positions of power also competed with the literati for the prestige associated with power, deploying a variety of cultural strategies, such as religious or artistic patronage, to present themselves as worthy of the trust and wealth they had come to hold from the emperors.

Kenneth J. Hammond is associate professor and chair of the Department of History at New Mexico State University. He is past president of the Society for Ming Studies.

On the sixteenth day of the seventh lunar month in the fourteenth year of the reign of Zhu Qizhen, the sixth emperor of the Ming dynasty, which by the Western calendar was the fourth of August, 1449, a grand military expedition departed the capital at Beijing through the Gate of Achieving Victory in the northern wall of the city. As the vanguard of this force headed out along the road that led to the Great Wall, and to the grasslands of Mongolia beyond the mountains that ranged north and west of Beijing, they passed between lines of officials from the imperial court, kneeling beside the road, prostrating themselves in the dirt, and wailing in protest. The officials did not want the emperor to undertake this

143

expedition. They had argued against it in the morning audiences at which the young emperor, just twenty-two years old, met with his Inner Court advisers. Many had submitted written memorials opposing it. Yet the emperor was indeed setting out on this summer morning to seek to punish the Oyirat Mongolian raiders, led by their new Khan Esen, who had been penetrating the Great Wall defense line and terrorizing the area near the capital.

The emperor's decision to launch this punitive expedition was influenced most decisively not by his Confucian ministers, but by an individual who was not even a member of the regular civil bureaucracy. He was Wang Zhen, the chief of the corps of eunuchs who staffed the Inner Palace, the residential compound of the ruler at the heart of the Forbidden City, the imperial palace that lay at the very center of Beijing—and symbolically at the center of the empire as well. By the middle years of the fifteenth century, eunuchs had come to wield significant power within the court of Zhu Qizhen. Wang Zhen was the greatest of these eunuchs, and he was able to overcome the opposition of the emperor's officials and induce the emperor to follow his guidance. How did he come to have this kind of power? And who and what were these eunuchs?

Eunuchs are men who have been castrated. In China, eunuchs first appear in history as victims of punishment for various crimes. Eunuchs are mentioned in the *Book of Odes* and *Book of Documents*, two of the classical texts that had their origins early in the first millennium B.C.E. Eunuchs are also discussed in the *Rites of Zhou*, which was believed by the Chinese to describe the organization of the Zhou state around the ninth century B.C.E. At first there were only a few eunuchs in the royal palace, and they were assigned to the most menial of tasks. The phrase "cleaning and sweeping" remained a common euphemism for the activities of eunuchs within the palace.

By the time of the Han dynasty (204 B.C.E. to 220 C.E.), both the number of eunuchs in the palace and the role they played had evolved. Castration was still a punishment inflicted on those who had violated the laws or offended the emperor, but by this time there were also eunuchs serving in the palace who were not convicted criminals. In some instances, young boys were offered by their families to the court, and if they were accepted they underwent the surgical removal of their genitals and, if they survived the operation, became servants of the emperor. This seems a rather harsh fate, but for poor families who could barely support themselves, it offered a way to guarantee their survival. Not only would the boy chosen for this role have a livelihood in the palace, but he would also be able to provide support for his family. Throughout the imperial era in China, many families chose this way to escape from poverty and starvation.

Still, eunuchs serving in the palace were intended to be servants, performing such tasks as cooking and cleaning, and not as part of the political establishment of the court. Why were eunuchs selected to work in the palace? The underlying reasons for this can be found in the cosmological ideas about nature and good government that formed the foundation for the whole Chinese imperial political order.

Early Chinese began to articulate their understanding of the way the universe worked in terms of the operation of two polar forces known as *yin* and *yang*. These were associated with linked phenomena like light and dark, warm and cold, day and night, the sun and the moon, male and female, and many others. All natural events and processes were seen as resulting from the interaction of these two primal elements. What was good and proper, whether in terms of the health of the body or the government of the empire, was based upon the proper balance, according to the particular circumstances of the moment, of these two forces.

The emperor was believed to be the embodiment of yang as a cosmic, creative force. Balancing this within the Inner Palace was the imperial harem, the women who resided in the Forbidden City. The emperor had one empress, but could have many consorts, sometimes even hundreds. These palace women formed a kind of reservoir of yin, to which only the emperor could have access. Other virile men, such as court officials, were not permitted to enter the Inner Palace, the private residence of the emperor.

Yet there were tasks which needed to be attended to in the Inner Palace, which it was felt the palace women and their female servants could or should not do. Eunuchs were seen as the only ones who could perform these functions. As castrated males, eunuchs were no longer seen as yang, but neither were they yin. And so they could live and work among the women of the Inner Palace without polluting or disturbing the proper balance of imperial yang and yin.

This close proximity of eunuchs to the daily lives of the emperors created the potential for problems as well. This was particularly true when young emperors came to the throne. Imperial princes, like boys in most traditional Chinese families, were raised in the Inner Quarters until they reached preadolescence. This meant that the strongest influences on them tended to be their mothers and other palace women, and sometimes eunuchs who waited on them. Princes, of course, were given instruction in the Confucian classical culture, but the court officials who were their tutors saw them only for limited times, while the women and eunuchs of the Inner Palace were their constant companions. Not surprisingly, when these young princes grew up and came to the throne, they sometimes still felt close bonds with their childhood eunuch associates.

Eunuchs were also sometimes seen as more reliable, or more dependent upon imperial favor, than regular officials. Court officials were drawn from the ranks of the educated Confucian elite and were often from families that owned land and had some economic base apart from employment in the government. Officials could have their own interests and agendas that did not necessarily coincide with those of the emperor. There could also be reasons of secrecy and security that might induce an emperor to use his eunuch retainers to carry messages or perform other tasks he did not want to entrust to regular officials.

In one way or another, eunuchs from time to time took on roles of political significance far beyond their original functions. As early as the seventh century B.C.E., the eunuch Shu Diao used his position within the court of the Duke of Qi to pursue his own political ambitions. Eunuchs such as Zhao Gao under the Qin (221–207 B.C.E.) and Cao Jie under the Han came to have great power and influence. Later, under the Tang dynasty (617–907 C.E.), eunuchs not only took on important powers at court, but also came to control military forces. A series of undistinguished emperors in the later years of the Tang allowed eunuchs to wield great power, which eventually triggered a reaction on the part of regular military and civil officials. In the Sweet Dew Incident of December 835, the emperor Wenzong attempted to crush the power of eunuchs who were dominating his court, but he was unable to do so and, instead, triggered a counterattack by Inner Palace eunuchs, whose military forces killed over a thousand regular Confucian officials and terrorized the Outer Court for years thereafter. Finally, in 903, a warlord named Zhu Quanzhong entered the Tang capital and slaughtered hundreds of eunuchs, effectively ending their control of the Tang court. Only four years later, the dynasty itself came to an end.

In the following Song dynasty (960–1279), and under the rule of the Mongol conquest dynasty called the Yuan (1271–1368), eunuchs were largely restricted to what was deemed to be their proper role as Inner Palace menial servants. When the Chinese peasant rebel Zhu Yuanzhang established the Ming dynasty in 1368, he proclaimed that eunuchs were to be kept in their lowly roles and explicitly forbade anyone to educate eunuchs, in order to prevent them from meddling in the documentary life of the government. Zhu Yuanzhang had a metal plaque set up in a courtyard in the imperial palace recording this prohibition and ordering eunuchs to refrain from involvement in politics.

Zhu Yuanzhang was a strong ruler, but also a paranoid one. He launched repeated attacks and purges against his Confucian officials. When he died in 1398, the succession became a controversial political issue. Zhu Yuanzhang had named his eldest son Zhu Biao as his heir, but he had died in 1392. Rather than name one of his other sons, Zhu Yuanzhang instead selected Zhu Biao's son Zhu Yunwen to be his successor. This upset the new emperor's uncles, especially Zhu Di, the Prince of Yan. But to make matters worse, Zhu Yunwen immediately set out to change many of the policies of his grandfather and, indeed, seemed intent on altering the whole political culture of the dynasty. Where Zhu Yuanzhang had called his reign period a time of "great martial virtue," Zhu Yunwen styled his own reign as a time for "fostering the civil [virtues]." He placed much greater faith in, and was much more reliant on, the Confucian officials.

Zhu Di resented his nephew's succession to the throne and saw his changes at court as a repudiation of the founder's legacy. In 1402 he launched a coup, and usurped the throne, becoming the third emperor of the Ming dynasty, known to history as the Yongle emperor. He carried out his coup from his base at the northern city of Yan, on the site of the modern city of Beijing. In planning and executing his campaign he began to utilize eunuchs from his princely court as secret agents, sending them to the imperial palace in Nanjing, supposedly on domestic tasks, but actually to gather information and engage in conspiratorial activities. He also began to use eunuchs to carry messages that he wanted to keep secure from the eyes and ears of Confucian officials whom, like his father, he did not fully trust. Even after his successful conquest of power, Zhu Di continued to use eunuchs in ways that violated the ban on eunuch involvement in politics, but that he found useful for his own purposes.

Zhu Di moved the capital of the Ming dynasty from the Yangtze River city of Nanjing to his own former princely seat, and the former capital of the Mongol Yuan dynasty, which became known as Beijing, or Northern Capital. He moved large numbers of artisans and craftsmen in, along with their families, to rebuild the city and construct the new imperial palaces, which still stand at the heart of the present-day capital of China. He shifted his administration there, and, by 1420, Beijing was functioning as the center of the empire.

Within the Inner Palace, Zhu Di made increasing use of eunuchs in handling minor administrative tasks. Casting aside the cautionary restrictions on eunuchs put in place by the founding emperor, one of Zhu Di's successors, the fifth Ming emperor Zhu Zhanji, in 1426, went so far as to establish the Inner Palace School, a training program for eunuchs that taught them to read and write to enable them to process many of the documents with which the emperor had to deal in his daily work. Eunuchs assumed increasingly important roles in handling the paperwork of the Ming government.

About the time that Zhu Di was preparing his coup against his nephew, a baby boy was born in the district of Yuzhou, in Shanxi province, southwest of Beijing. Details of his early life, and even the exact date of his birth, are unknown. He was named Wang Zhen, and he would come to be one of the most powerful eunuchs in Chinese history.

Unlike the vast majority of eunuchs in the Ming and other dynasties, it appears that Wang Zhen was not castrated as a little boy, but rather underwent the operation as a young man. He had received a regular Confucian education, and his family probably had ambitions for him to achieve success in the Confucian examination system, the principal means for entering government service in the later imperial era. We do not know for certain, but it may be that Wang Zhen attempted to pass the very lowest level of the examinations without success and then decided to follow an alternative course to work within the imperial palace.

When the Inner Palace School was being set up in 1426, there was a need for instructors who could work within the residential area of the Forbidden City. Wang Zhen was recruited for this purpose. He first was given assignments as a teacher for some of the palace women. He also taught and served as an administrator for the Inner Palace School. But his real break came when, on the basis of his Confucian education and his previous performance as an instructor within the palace, he was named as tutor to one of the imperial princes, Zhu Qizhen. In 1435, Zhu Zhanji died, and Zhu Qizhen ascended the throne as the new emperor. He was eight years old.

This was a classic situation that provided Wang Zhen with a great deal of influence over the boy emperor. Zhu Qizhen naturally looked to Wang for advice and guidance. He was on familiar terms with Wang, but was not comfortable with the Confucian officials of the Outer Court, which was dominated at this time by three senior Grand Secretaries, the highest post in the Ming civil administration. All three of these men shared the surname Yang, though they were not related to one another. The Three Yangs, as they were commonly known, were Yang Shiqi, Yang Rong, and Yang Pu. They had risen in government service under the Yongle emperor, and by then were old and experienced politicians. They naturally assumed a leading role in guiding the young ruler in taking up his duties.

The young emperor was also close to his grandmother, the dowager empress Zhang. Though her husband Zhu Gaozhi had died after reigning as emperor for only a short time, from January to May 1425, she had remained an important figure at court, first guiding her son Zhu Zhanji as emperor and then as a moral instructress for her grandson.

Early in the reign of Zhu Qizhen, Wang Zhen attempted to undermine one of the leading court officials, a man named Zhang Fu. Wang Zhen privately accused Zhang Fu of corruption in his administration of the Confucian examination system and had Zhang dismissed from his posts in the government. The dowager empress asked the boy emperor why he had done this. Upon learning that it was Wang Zhen who had instigated the affair, she was furious. She informed the Three Yangs, who wanted to do away with Wang. Only the pleading of her grandson saved Wang Zhen from being executed. Zhang Fu was restored to his former positions. Wang Zhen learned to fear the power of the dowager empress and the senior Grand Secretaries. He refrained from further efforts to manipulate the political scene for the time being.

Over the next few years, Wang worked on developing a base of political support in the Outer Court. One significant way in which he pursued this was through making recommendations to the emperor regarding candidates for government offices. Men aspiring to high positions began to cultivate Wang Zhen's favor, and he was able to build up a network of relationships and obligations with rising Confucian officials. For example, he supported the careers of Xu Xi, who became minister of war in 1442, and Wang You, who was named vice minister of works in 1441. Wang Zhen was also able to develop support in the Embroidered Uniform Guard, a special military unit, which provided the personal bodyguard for the emperor and also performed secret police functions throughout the empire. Wang allied himself with Ma Shun, who became commander of the Embroidered Uniform Guard. In 1442 he was able to secure an appointment as a vice commander in the guard for his nephew, Wang Shan, and later, in 1446, another nephew, Wang Lin, was also made an assistant commander. Thus, through a combination of patronage of regular Confucian officials and placement of members of his family in powerful military posts, Wang Zhen extended his power from the Inner Palace to the broader political arena.

It was also during these years in the early 1440s that Wang Zhen began to pursue another strategy to enhance his status and prestige. He became a patron of Buddhism. Buddhism was an important religion in the Ming dynasty, especially in the capital at Beijing. The Yongle emperor, Zhu Di, had been a great patron, especially of Tibetan Buddhism. Many temples and monasteries had been built in the new capital, and older ones had been restored. In the first century or so of the Ming period, the Confucian literati had not been major devotees of Buddhism, although this would change later in the dynasty. In the middle years of the fifteenth century, many eunuchs, as they rose to positions of power and accumulated wealth, began to contribute to the building of temples or the restoration of old ones. A number of these eunuch-sponsored temples remain in Beijing today, including the one built by Wang Zhen.

This temple, called the Zhihua si, or the Temple of Transforming Wisdom, was built on the east side of the city, near one of the large granaries where tribute from southern China was stored to feed the troops stationed at the capital. The Zhihua si is a medium-sized temple, with three courtyards and a two-storied Hall of Ten Thousand Buddhas as its most prominent feature. Wang Zhen had a private residence for himself built next to the temple and used both the residence and the temple to host gatherings of friends and political cronies. Indeed, he even moved a troupe of musicians from the court into the temple to provide music for the monks' ritual activities and used the same musicians to perform at social gatherings. He added some performers from his hometown in Shanxi, and the Zhihua si developed a unique musical style that became quite famous. Even today, this musical tradition survives among a small group of former monks and young students who give public performances at the temple.

There was a special attraction in Buddhism for eunuchs. In the Confucian teachings upon which the orthodox order of the literati officials was based, reverence for one's ancestors was a central virtue. The physical body that one received from one's parents was in effect a gift from the ancestors to be preserved as best one could. Eunuchs, as individuals who had undergone physical mutilation, were seen as morally deformed as well. Furthermore, by enduring castration, eunuchs abdicated the duty to perpetuate their family lines and therefore excluded themselves from the rituals of ancestor worship and family morality. Buddhist monks and nuns, who took vows of celibacy and left their families to live in monastic communities, were likewise seen as outside the proper moral order of the family by many Confucians. This shared outsider status seems to have engendered a sympathy between eunuchs and Buddhism.

By engaging in conspicuous actions of public patronage of the Zhihua si, Wang Zhen was presenting himself as a kind of surrogate for imperial patronage. Emperors and other members of the imperial family routinely endowed temples and gave lavish presents to monasteries. In effect, Wang Zhen was claiming for himself, as were other eunuchs at this time, a greater degree of legitimacy in the public eye. As some eunuchs achieved power and influence at court, it seemed natural to them that they should also be seen as capable of acts of religious patronage. This provided them with a kind of cultural capital that further enhanced their ability to operate in the political realm of the Outer Court.

This strategy was not by any means always successful. For the most part, Confucian officials of the literati class continued to view the eunuchs very negatively. They might be driven from time to time to seek political advantage by allying themselves with one or another prominent eunuch, but they did so without ever seeing the eunuchs as their equals. Many literati refused to have anything to do with eunuchs, even when it would have been to their political advantage to enter into tactical alliances. A classic example of this was Xue Xuan, who came from the same locality as Wang Zhen, and became a rising official, serving as a provincial-level education commissioner in Shandong in the late 1430s. Wang Zhen wanted to promote men from his native place to high positions, in the hopes of building close political links with them. In 1441 he had Xue Xuan named vice minister of the Grand Court of Revision, a prominent literary post in the capital. Other high officials urged Xue to pay a courtesy call on Wang Zhen to thank him, but Xue declined to do so. In a famous encounter, he met Wang Zhen in one of the halls of the palace and merely bowed to him, while other officials dropped to their knees. Because Xue Xuan would not accept his efforts to recruit him as a close associate, Wang Zhen developed a strong hatred for Xue. He contrived to have him arrested and sentenced to death. Xue was only saved by the lucky actions of Wang Zhen's cook, who was from the home region of Wang and Xue. Wang Zhen saw the cook weeping and asked him why, to which the cook replied that he was sad that Mr. Xue was to be executed. When he explained that he felt close to Xue because of their shared native place, Wang Zhen relented and spared Xue's life. But it was only after Wang Zhen's death that Xue was able to return to his official career.

By the mid-1440s, Wang Zhen was able to emerge as perhaps the most powerful individual in the empire. All three of the Grand Secretaries who had led the Outer Court in the first years of Zhu Qizhen's reign died in the early 1440s, as did the young emperor's grandmother. No truly powerful figure was left to counter Wang Zhen's influence. When Zhu Qizhen became a young man, turning eighteen in 1445, he was eager to rule in his own right, and he adopted a lofty, sometimes arrogant attitude toward the Confucian officials. But he still remained very close to Wang Zhen, relying on him for advice and counsel. Without the restraints imposed by the Three Yangs and Dowager Empress Zhang, Wang Zhen could now enhance his own power and guide the emperor as he thought best.

Drawing on the network of allies he had built up, including Xu Xi and Wang You in the Outer Court, and Ma Shun and his nephew Wang Shan in the Embroidered Uniform Guard, Wang Zhen began to pursue policies that the Three Yangs and Dowager Empress Zhang had opposed, but about which the emperor was enthusiastic. Perhaps most important among these was a major military campaign on the southwestern border. There was a three-way conflict of interests among the Chinese, the local Shan people, and the Burmese kingdom farther south over this venture. In the 1440s, this set of conflicts came to focus on an area called Luchuan, where a Shan leader named Thonganbwa was striving to consolidate power. In 1441 and again in 1443–44, the Chinese launched major offensives, under the command of Wang Ji, an ally of Wang Zhen.

These were eventually successful to some degree, with the Burmese handing over the body of Thonganbwa to the Chinese in 1446. But Thonganbwa's son carried on resistance to the Chinese, and the situation by the late 1440s remained unresolved.

These campaigns were the subject of much debate at the Ming court. The version of history that became officially sanctioned reflects the consensus of later Confucian officials and generally portrays Wang Zhen as having promoted these campaigns as military adventures to enhance his own power. The campaigns drained the imperial treasury and diverted resources from the northern borderlands, where the Mongols remained a more active threat. But the conduct of military actions along China's frontiers was a well-established aspect of Ming policy, with the Yongle emperor Zhu Di the model of a strong and aggressive leader who sought to expand and consolidate Ming power along both northern and southern borders. Wang Zhen's advocacy of military action was not inconsistent with Ming practice. And the emperor, Zhu Qizhen, seems to have been very much interested in emulating his imperial ancestor Zhu Di.

One official who opposed the Luchuan campaigns was Liu Qiu, who worked in the imperial think tank, the Hanlin Academy. He submitted a lengthy memorial in which he not only expressed his concerns about military issues in the southwest, but also subtly implied that the emperor was allowing Wang Zhen too much power and control over court affairs. Wang Zhen clearly saw this as an attack on his position and moved to discredit Liu, who was arrested and then executed by the Embroidered Uniform Guard. This kind of harsh suppression of his enemies was effective in giving Wang Zhen even greater dominance over the emperor.

Ironically, while many of Wang Zhen's critics opposed the southwestern military campaigns on the grounds that they undermined security along the northern frontier, when Wang began to propose a major military expedition to deal with the Mongol threat in 1449, the same officials also came out against this venture. The Mongols had become a more pressing concern as a new leader had emerged among them. Esen, Khan of the Oyirat tribes, had begun to lead raids across the Great Wall, which at this time was not in good repair and hence constituted a less than formidable barrier.

The Yongle emperor had carried out a series of four major expeditions against the Mongols beyond the Great Wall in the 1410s and 1420s, driving them far from China's immediate frontiers and into the grasslands. This aggressive approach to dealing with the Mongols was seen by Yongle as consistent with the stance of his father, the dynastic founder Zhu Yuanzhang, and with the overall martial tenor of the early Ming monarchy. But in the years since the death of the Yongle emperor in 1424, the political culture of the dynasty had developed in the direction of dominance on the part of the civil Confucian officials, and away from the military activism of the early reigns. Thus official opposition to renewed, imperially led campaigns beyond the Great Wall had a basis in a general antipathy toward the military aspect of government, as well as a specific antagonism between Confucian scholars and eunuchs.

Wang Zhen saw his advocacy of an anti-Mongol campaign as consistent with earlier Ming practice and as an opportunity for his protégé, the still young emperor Zhu Qizhen, to establish himself as a worthy successor to his great-grandfather Zhu Di, the Yongle emperor. Although Wang has been portrayed as evil and corrupt by Confucian historians, his actions can be seen as reasonable in the context of the times.

As this chapter opened, when the emperor led his forces out from Beijing in August 1449, Confucian officials knelt beside the road, wailing and expressing their opposition to the campaign. As things actually turned out, their concerns were well founded.

The imperial forces marched out through the pass in the Great Wall and onto the open terrain beyond, but they were unable to make effective contact with the Mongols. Scouts reported that the Mongols were gathering a major force to counter the imperial army, and rather than risk an engagement far from their base area, the Chinese column turned back toward the capital. The details of what ensued have been obscured and distorted through various biases on the part of subsequent Confucian historians. At the least, we know that on September 1, 1449, the Chinese army camped at a place called Tumu, the last stopping point before its return through the Great Wall northwest of Beijing. (It has been alleged that the army stopped at this point in order to wait for Wang Zhen's personal baggage train to catch up, but this may be a later invention.)

The Mongol forces fell upon the imperial troops at Tumu, and in a complete rout, the Chinese were killed or driven off in great numbers. Wang Zhen died, although there is a strong tradition that he was killed by his own men rather than the Mongols. The worst outcome of the Battle of Tumu was that the emperor was captured by the Mongols and carried off by them into their homeland. He was held prisoner for a year before being ransomed in September 1450. By that time his younger brother, Zhu Qiyou, had been placed on the throne by a coalition of Confucian officials and eunuchs who had been jealous of Wang Zhen's prominence. Even after Zhu Qizhen was ransomed, he was not allowed to resume the throne, but was kept under a kind of house arrest in a palace in Beijing for the next seven years. Eventually he was able to assemble a new alliance of officials and eunuchs of his own, and in 1457, he overthrew his brother and reclaimed the throne. He then reigned until his death in February 1464.

Immediately after the disaster at Tumu in 1449, Wang Zhen had been officially disgraced. There had been open conflict between those in the palace who remained loyal to Wang Zhen and those who wished to eradicate all traces of his influence. Before long, the anti-Wang forces triumphed, his property was confiscated, and many of his relatives and supporters were executed, including his nephews in the Embroidered Uniform Guard and the Guard Commander Ma Shun. Wang was officially blamed not only for the failure of the military campaign against the Mongols but for every other shortcoming of the imperial regime.

When Zhu Qizhen retook the throne in 1457, however, he at once set out to honor Wang Zhen's memory. As emperor, he remained devoted to his former tutor. He had a shrine to Wang built at the Zhihua si, the Buddhist temple in eastern Beijing that had been Wang's home, with sacrifices to Wang's spirit carried out under imperial patronage. This shrine remained active for the rest of the Ming dynasty, and even into the succeeding Qing dynasty, until 1742, when it was destroyed after a junior official denounced the sacrifices to Wang Zhen as honoring an evil eunuch. Today the Zhihua si still stands, and the stone tablet with an image of Wang Zhen can still be seen within the temple grounds.

The death of Wang Zhen in 1449 brought to an end the career of the first of the truly powerful eunuchs of the Ming dynasty. He had maximized the political advantages to be had from his position as tutor to the heir apparent, and positioned himself as the emperor's most trusted adviser when young Zhu Qizhen assumed the throne in 1435. Posthumously he has become symbolic of the eunuchs' abuse of power, which came to be seen as characteristic of the Ming dynasty. He is often labeled as the first of the "four great evil eunuchs," a group that also includes Wang Zhi, Liu Jin, and Wei Zhongxian. It has been a standard assumption of Confucian historians that the power exercised by these and other eunuchs was illegitimate, and that the ends they sought were by definition corrupt. Given the almost total monopoly on historical discourse held by the Confucian elite, it is very difficult to reconstruct any kind of sympathetic account of Wang Zhen's life and career. And yet it is possible, by considering his actions in the context of political and cultural precedents and the context of the mid-fifteenth century, to see him at least as someone who acted within the established norms of the dynasty, and who sought to serve his emperor loyally.

SUGGESTED READINGS

Brook, Timothy. *The Confusions of Pleasure: Commerce and Culture in Ming China*. Berkeley, 1998.

Dreyer, Edward L. *Early Ming China: A Political History, 1355-1435*. Stanford, 1982.

Tsai, Shih-shan Henry. *The Eunuchs in the Ming Dynasty*. Albany, 1996.

CHAPTER 10

The Merchant Wang Zhen

1424–1495

INA ASIM

Ming society grew even more complicated as the commercial sector of the economy revived and resumed the dynamic expansion that had begun in the Southern Song, only to be disrupted by the era of Mongol conquest and rule. Now commercial wealth began to be accumulated by families who sought to establish themselves as the social and cultural equals of the traditional literati elite. As the story of Wang Zhen (whose name is pronounced like that of the eunuch in the previous chapter, but who is entirely unrelated to him) shows us, merchants in the Ming could achieve great things, and merchant families could find ways to enter into the very heart of elite culture through the Confucian examination system.

Ina Asim, assistant professor at the Institute of Sinology at the University of Würzberg, Germany, uses both textual and other material sources from the recent archaeological excavation of Wang's tomb to construct a portrait of Wang and his family that gives us some insight into this rising class and the challenges its members faced in a period of rapid change. Although the conflict between commercial elites and preexisting agrarian aristocracies drove much of early modern European social and economic history, China seems to have taken a somewhat different path. The interplay of economic, social, and cultural forces in the Ming dynasty is a subject requiring much more study, and it brings us to the threshold of the modern period in China as well.

In general, little is known about the individual lives of merchants prior to the Song dynasty (960–1279), the period in which this social class gained considerably in importance. Even when the commercial sector of the Chinese economy began to expand again after the Ming dynasty (1368–1644) was firmly established, biographical information about merchants was most commonly related only in casual entries in journals or other records of personal observations written by officials or literati. A merchant may perhaps have been the model for a character in a theater play or in a piece of fiction, forms of literature that grew increasingly popular in the sixteenth century, but rarely do we find authentic biographical data on merchants in early modern China. If attracted by the idea of expounding their thoughts to a larger public, merchants themselves generally preferred to give instructions on how to conduct business properly, how to act in conformity with leading Confucian values, successful business administration, or on philanthropic patronage of the arts. Richard John Lufrano, in his *Honorable Merchants: Commerce and Self-Cultivation in Late Imperial China*, mentions several works by merchants who published their professional ideas or ethical beliefs, carefully situating themselves within a Confucian public discourse that they hoped would legitimize their commercial activities.

Yet some kinds of biographical materials do exist that reveal not only information about a single individual, but, as with the present subject, can also serve as indicators of the extent to which transgressing existing social conventions by merchants was acceptable in the social matrix of the Ming dynasty. One type of such biographical material is preserved in inscriptions on stone funereal tablets, the praises of the deceased that were placed inside his or her tomb. An exclusive document by definition, the honor of being given such a tablet was in theory granted only to officials, their wives, and their parents. But when excavated, some of these tablets, which usually have been hidden for centuries in the protective seclusion of the graves, reveal surprising facts. They can be used to investigate, and in many cases reevaluate, established social theories and historical ideas based on more commonly accepted written sources. One such inscription comes from an archaeological find that has been the source of spectacular objects and a wealth of other information, the tomb for the joint burial of the wealthy merchant Wang Zhen and his wife, Mme Liu (1425–1503, buried 1505). It is in the county seat of prosperous Huaian County in Jiangsu province, a commercial town on the banks of the Grand Canal. Their tomb allows us to travel back in time and reconstruct aspects of their lifestyle that provide us with more precise biographical data than the usual eulogy that has survived in a friend's writings.

Wang Zhen died at the age of seventy-two *sui*, after a life full of wealth and luxury, based on a fortune accumulated by his grandfather, his father, and to a certain degree by himself. His wife, Mme Liu, had given birth to four sons who survived the difficult days of childhood and grew up diligently studying the Confucian classics. Their aim was to participate in the official examinations, which might have opened a career in the bureaucracy for them. In those days, the formula for economic success and social prestige was composed of the two elements of official position and money. Being appointed to an official post was still the most desired and respected goal in an educated man's life. And since merchants had become an increasingly important part of a functional symbiosis with the ruling bureaucratic and aristocratic elites, the dilemma of the contradiction between money and official service was solved by the merchant family clans in a pragmatic way. They sent their academically talented male youths to school in the hope that tutoring by a learned scholar would instill a hunger for erudition in them and set them on the track of a successful scholarly career. Those sons who were considered more apt to directly enhance the family's material prosperity were introduced to the ways of merchants or initiated into the skills of artisans, according to the respective family trade. Clans whose young men eventually proved successful, either in their official career or in business, could follow the strategy of concentrating private finances and administrative power. The clan could rely on favorable decisions by clan members who were officials because they were acquainted with economic processes. In the same way, officials could count on kinship support in times of need.

Before the Ming dynasty, this exchange would not have been an option, as not only the sons but even the grandsons of merchants were banned from taking the examinations. In Confucian culture there had been a hierarchy of classes within which merchants occupied the lowest rung and were viewed as unacceptable as candidates for public office. Members of the *shi* literati elite were ranked highest, followed by peasants, who grew the food everyone needed to live, and artisans, who produced useful objects for daily life. Merchants were seen as social parasites. But as commercial wealth grew more significant, beginning in the Song period and then with even greater force in the Ming, merchant families asserted claims to social and cultural legitimacy, which eventually resulted in the barriers to the examinations being lowered, although they were never completely removed. In the Ming, sons of merchants were granted the right to sit for the exams, but no one who was actually engaged in commerce as a livelihood could do so.

Wang Zhen had been no exception to the standard career pattern. His father and his uncle devotedly enhanced the family's prosperity through trade, and they initially made Wang Zhen enter the ranks of grain merchants, sometime between 1450 and 1456. Feeling rather different from his elders, Wang Zhen disliked this kind of work. Having been exposed to the classics in his childhood, he was inclined toward the arts. He loved books, calligraphy, and paintings, and, over time, while spending a fortune on a collection of ancient and contemporary paintings and calligraphy, he became an expert in distinguishing genuine works of art from copies and fakes. With like-minded devotees he would spend his time in reclusion and in discussion of the finer specimens of his collection. His biographer also informs us that he did not love only the serious world of the literati, but craved the most exclusive and sophisticated objects and was eager to include them in his treasuries. Wang Zhen's son also tells us in his tomb inscription, which had been placed on top of the outer coffin within the grave, that his father was also known to have appreciated the pleasures of female company and the delightful flavors of food and delicacies. When times got rough for those in his neighborhood who did not enjoy such blessed conditions in life, he proved to be a philanthropist who not only knew how to live but also how to give. He followed this cause of supporting people in need through several famine relief efforts during the half-century between 1437 and 1487.

He himself did not force his four sons to follow mercantile professions, but instead he tried to lead them to a scholar's life, an effort which in the end was to no avail. Only in the generation of his grandsons, when three of the eight young men became officials, did this dream come into being. Yet their ranks are not mentioned in the tomb inscription of Mme Liu, who was buried next to her husband in 1505, ten years after he had died. We must assume that at the time their influence did not yet extend beyond the local level. Unfortunately, Wang Zhen did not live to see his grandsons' professional success. They must have been still too young at his death, for they were not mentioned in his tomb inscription at all. But we do learn about his sons. His eldest son, Xi, who composed the tomb inscriptions for his parents, was followed by Zhen, and their younger brothers Qi and Lu. Only three of them may have attended the funeral of their father as obedient sons must. Qi, who had been a successful student and had passed the local and midlevel examinations in 1489, went to the capital as a provincial graduate, in order to take the metropolitan examination. But Wang Zhen did not have the satisfaction of seeing him enter on an official career, because Qi and his wife, Mme Chen, died there of unknown causes. His wife's last name is identical with the last names of Xi's wife and the second wife of Zhen. It is not clear whether the Chen family with whom the Wangs sought to tighten their alliance through marriage ties was from the same clan. The brothers may have been married to sisters or cousins from the Chen clan, yet their wives may also have been from different clans with the name of Chen. Zhen's first wife was a Mme Liang, and the youngest of the four brothers married a Mme Yang, and, after her untimely death, a Mme Lu.

The marriage strategy for the four daughters of Wang Zhen and Mme Liu seems to have been designed to bring several different families into close relationships with the Wangs: Shuqing married Shen Yue, who died early. Her sister Shujing married Tao Hong. Unfortunately, fate did not grant them a long, happy marriage either, because Shujing died at some point between 1496 and 1505. The third daughter Shulian wed Xu

Ang, and the youngest, Shuji, married Shi Ce, who died before 1505. We are told that the families of this second generation had six grandsons and three granddaughters to lay in the arms of grandfather Wang Zhen. (By 1505, the burial year of Mme Liu, one grandson must have died and a fourth granddaughter been born, because different numbers of grandchildren are recorded on her tablet.)

According to burial regulations, neither Wang Zhen nor his wife was entitled to receive a tomb inscription, because Wang Zhen himself had been neither a member of the aristocracy nor an official, nor had one of his sons, by virtue of official rank, obtained the right to confer a title upon his deceased father. Therefore, in the head of the inscription, Wang Zhen is politely referred to as an "unemployed scholar." The Wangs' belonging to a social class that was still denied such privileges as tomb inscriptions did not stop the clan members from using this powerful symbol of status to provide their deceased with the means to demonstrate their position in the netherworld. Just like her husband, Mme Liu was honored with an inscription tablet by her son Xi, which was also carved by someone named Wang, supposedly a relative. Mme Liu's father had belonged to one of the old families of Shanyang County. We are told that he lived as a recluse and studied for his personal enjoyment and self-improvement, a modest description of a lifestyle that was based on substantial financial resources. When his daughter was nineteen she married Wang Zhen and served him, his parents, and his uncle as devotedly as was to be expected from an obedient daughter-in-law. Her temperament is described as peace-loving, honest, and sharing. She is said to have cared for the elders in the family with just as much diligence as she displayed in caring for her four sons, four daughters, five grandsons, four granddaughters, two great-grandsons, and one great-granddaughter. She was a perfect host to the family's guests and set herself to keeping everything in the household clean and tidy. Though she did not understand much of the Confucian classics or literati arts such as painting, she devotedly studied Buddhist scriptures.

Although it must be assumed that it was more common to neglect the regulations for the rites of passage than the written sources generally make us believe, the fact that Wang Zhen and his wife were given tomb inscriptions is still rather unusual among excavated tombs. But there are even more striking features indicating the extraordinary position of this merchant family. The Wang clan took special care with regard to the equipment buried in the tomb for the use of Wang Zhen in his capacity as the deceased head of their clan. He was given a selection of thirty everyday utensils, which were supposed to serve him in the netherworld as the ones at his disposal had served him in life. Among the objects, which were stored in the outer sandalwood coffin and had remained in excellent condition until the day of their excavation, were four cotton quilts, eight outer garments (including cloud-patterned silk gowns with long sleeves, plain white cotton shirts with long sleeves, a cotton-padded jacket made of yellow silk), six inner garments (including a plain white skirt, plain cotton-padded silk pants, plain white cotton pants, and plain white-lined pants), three pairs of boot stockings, and a pair of long white stockings. Wang was also given a ceramic jar, a basket woven from bamboo, two green-glazed bowls, a golden earpick, and a pair of chopsticks.

In addition to these mundane objects, two wooden rosaries and five coin-size gold tin plates with long-life blessings as well as his most cherished paintings and calligraphies by well-known Yuan and early Ming painters accompanied him into the next world. The paintings were to please his spirit as they had delighted him ever since he had added them to his collection. These textiles and paintings are special highlights among Wang's burial objects, and they make his tomb a treasure of material culture, providing a unique contribution to understanding one individual from a class that had only recently emerged from social inferiority to a more prestigious and honored position.

The image of Wang Zhen gained from tomb inscriptions and burial objects has been further enhanced by a very particular phenomenon. When the inner coffin of Wang Zhen was opened, his body was found in a perfectly preserved condition, probably due to the insulating effects of a paste mixed from lime and glutinous rice deposited around the outer coffin and putty between inner and outer coffin. With his hair and skin intact and his joints movable, the five hundred years that had elapsed between Wang Zhen's death and his discovery by the archaeologists who excavated his tomb, melted to a mere moment. Here was an individual who, by well-considered management of the blessings that fate had conferred upon him, had formed his life according to his needs and desires, a life that, despite social sanctions, had favored a merchant over many officials of equal or even higher standing who had to fight the vicissitudes of politics. The quality of preservation that he was able to afford at the end of his life allowed his mortal remains to survive long after his spirit had departed. For the archaeologists working on this excavation, it was a remarkable instance of a direct encounter with an individual from the past.

Wang Zhen's tomb inscription reads as follows:

> Tomb inscription of the unemployed scholar Mr Wang, with the taboo name Bo'an, whose ancestors had been from Yizhou County in Yangzhou [prefecture]. Since the Hongwu reign period (1368–1398) his grandfather had been registered in Huai'an, where he built a house for the family. [His

great-grandfather's] taboo name was Wen. His mother was from the Ling clan, and he was born on the 12th day of the 10th month of the *jiazhen* year of the reign of the Yongle emperor [1424].

He was of a pure and good-hearted natural disposition. Simple and sincere, from his childhood on he studied according to the Principles [of Confucian teaching]. Following his nature, he was not fond of extravagance.

His father and his uncle were devoted to enhancing the family's prosperity through trade and there was property in abundance. In the Jingtai reign period (1450–1456), he entered the ranks of the grain merchants. Again and again he took leave and did not want to come back [to this work], and he left it to his younger brother to watch over the hundred households of guards. [Instead] he became a judicial clerk. He managed domestic affairs in a diligent and frugal fashion. He had his ways of making money, from which his family could increase its wealth. In the Tianshun (1437–1464) and Chenghua (1465–1487) reigns he repeatedly organized famine relief measures without receiving any official assistance and support.

His most cherished matters of heart were ancient and contemporary calligraphies and ink paintings. Until the day of his death he opened and read [scrolls of calligraphy and painting] and found incessant pleasure in them without ever losing his interest. He rejoiced in the pleasures of female company as well as in the delightful flavors of delicacies. He was extraordinarily versed in judging whether a painting was genuine or fake. The top paintings in his collection were truly priceless.

In his later years he increasingly loved to rest with a few close friends, and refrained from teaching his sons, who have all grown up.

Zhangxi managed the household.

Cizhen administered [the family's affairs] according to the *Book of Rites*. Between 1477 and 1480, he participated repeatedly in the examinations in the Southern Capital without receiving a degree.

Ciqi in 1489 was recruited by regular examination as provincial graduate in the metropolitan examination for the Ministry of Rites. He died in the capital.

Cilu was appointed National University Student.

On the 22nd day of the seventh month of the year 1495, Wang Zhen died in his death chamber at the age of 72 *sui*. On the sixth day of the first month of the following year (1496) he was buried in his family tomb outside Dongmen Gate.

He had been married to Mme Liu from the same home [district]. The daughter and sons [and their spouses] were the following: the four sons: Zhangxi married Mme Chen, Cizhen married Mme Liang and Mme Chen, Ciqi married Mme Chen, and Cilu married Mme Yang and Mme Lu. The four daughters: Shuqing got married to Shen Yue; Shujing got married to Tao Hong; Shulian got married to Xu Ang; Shuji got married to Shi Ce. Of the six grandsons Jianzhong was engaged to Mlle Hang, Zhizhong was engaged to Mlle Ye. Dezhong was introduced to the daughters no. 4, no. 5, and no. 6 of the Han family but was not engaged to any of them. Of the three granddaughters the eldest was betrothed to Yang Zhen, the second was betrothed to Bi Jing, the third was not betrothed at all. Carved on the sixth day of the first month of the *bingchen* year of the Hongzhi reign (1496) by Wang Bi from Shanyang.

SUGGESTED READINGS

Brokaw, Cynthia J. *The Ledgers of Merit and Demerit: Social Change and Moral Order in Late Imperial China*. Princeton, 1991.

Gates, Hill. *China's Motor: A Thousand Years of Petty Capitalism*. Ithaca, NY, 1996.

Lufrano, Richard John. *Honorable Merchants: Commerce and Self-Cultivation in Late Imperial China*. Honolulu, 1997.

Von Glahn, Richard. *Fountain of Fortune: Money and Monetary Policy in China, 1000–1700*. Berkeley, 1996.

Web Sites

CHINA: A COUNTRY STUDY
http://lcweb2.loc.gov/frd/cs/cntoc.html

ANCIENT EAST ASIA
www.AncientEastAsia.com

HISTORY OF CHINA
www.chaos.umd.edu/history/time_line.html

CHINA
www.infoplease.com/ipa/A0107411.html

Index

167